The victim of prejudice. In two volumes. By Mary Hays, author of The memoirs of Emma Courtney. ... Volume 1 of 2

Mary Hays

PRINT EDITIONS

Eighteenth Century
Collections Online
Print Editions

Gale ECCO Print Editions

Relive history with *Eighteenth Century Collections Online*, now available in print for the independent historian and collector. This series includes the most significant English-language and foreign-language works printed in Great Britain during the eighteenth century, and is organized in seven different subject areas including literature and language; medicine, science, and technology; and religion and philosophy. The collection also includes thousands of important works from the Americas.

The eighteenth century has been called "The Age of Enlightenment." It was a period of rapid advance in print culture and publishing, in world exploration, and in the rapid growth of science and technology – all of which had a profound impact on the political and cultural landscape. At the end of the century the American Revolution, French Revolution and Industrial Revolution, perhaps three of the most significant events in modern history, set in motion developments that eventually dominated world political, economic, and social life.

In a groundbreaking effort, Gale initiated a revolution of its own: digitization of epic proportions to preserve these invaluable works in the largest online archive of its kind. Contributions from major world libraries constitute over 175,000 original printed works. Scanned images of the actual pages, rather than transcriptions, recreate the works *as they first appeared.*

Now for the first time, these high-quality digital scans of original works are available via print-on-demand, making them readily accessible to libraries, students, independent scholars, and readers of all ages.

For our initial release we have created seven robust collections to form one the world's most comprehensive catalogs of 18th century works.

Initial Gale ECCO Print Editions collections include:

History and Geography
Rich in titles on English life and social history, this collection spans the world as it was known to eighteenth-century historians and explorers. Titles include a wealth of travel accounts and diaries, histories of nations from throughout the world, and maps and charts of a world that was still being discovered. Students of the War of American Independence will find fascinating accounts from the British side of conflict.

Social Science
Delve into what it was like to live during the eighteenth century by reading the first-hand accounts of everyday people, including city dwellers and farmers, businessmen and bankers, artisans and merchants, artists and their patrons, politicians and their constituents. Original texts make the American, French, and Industrial revolutions vividly contemporary.

Medicine, Science and Technology
Medical theory and practice of the 1700s developed rapidly, as is evidenced by the extensive collection, which includes descriptions of diseases, their conditions, and treatments. Books on science and technology, agriculture, military technology, natural philosophy, even cookbooks, are all contained here.

Literature and Language
Western literary study flows out of eighteenth-century works by Alexander Pope, Daniel Defoe, Henry Fielding, Frances Burney, Denis Diderot, Johann Gottfried Herder, Johann Wolfgang von Goethe, and others. Experience the birth of the modern novel, or compare the development of language using dictionaries and grammar discourses.

Religion and Philosophy
The Age of Enlightenment profoundly enriched religious and philosophical understanding and continues to influence present-day thinking. Works collected here include masterpieces by David Hume, Immanuel Kant, and Jean-Jacques Rousseau, as well as religious sermons and moral debates on the issues of the day, such as the slave trade. The Age of Reason saw conflict between Protestantism and Catholicism transformed into one between faith and logic -- a debate that continues in the twenty-first century.

Law and Reference
This collection reveals the history of English common law and Empire law in a vastly changing world of British expansion. Dominating the legal field is the *Commentaries of the Law of England* by Sir William Blackstone, which first appeared in 1765. Reference works such as almanacs and catalogues continue to educate us by revealing the day-to-day workings of society.

Fine Arts
The eighteenth-century fascination with Greek and Roman antiquity followed the systematic excavation of the ruins at Pompeii and Herculaneum in southern Italy; and after 1750 a neoclassical style dominated all artistic fields. The titles here trace developments in mostly English-language works on painting, sculpture, architecture, music, theater, and other disciplines. Instructional works on musical instruments, catalogs of art objects, comic operas, and more are also included.

The BiblioLife Network

This project was made possible in part by the BiblioLife Network (BLN), a project aimed at addressing some of the huge challenges facing book preservationists around the world. The BLN includes libraries, library networks, archives, subject matter experts, online communities and library service providers. We believe every book ever published should be available as a high-quality print reproduction; printed on-demand anywhere in the world. This insures the ongoing accessibility of the content and helps generate sustainable revenue for the libraries and organizations that work to preserve these important materials.

The following book is in the "public domain" and represents an authentic reproduction of the text as printed by the original publisher. While we have attempted to accurately maintain the integrity of the original work, there are sometimes problems with the original work or the micro-film from which the books were digitized. This can result in minor errors in reproduction. Possible imperfections include missing and blurred pages, poor pictures, markings and other reproduction issues beyond our control. Because this work is culturally important, we have made it available as part of our commitment to protecting, preserving, and promoting the world's literature.

GUIDE TO FOLD-OUTS MAPS and OVERSIZED IMAGES

The book you are reading was digitized from microfilm captured over the past thirty to forty years. Years after the creation of the original microfilm, the book was converted to digital files and made available in an online database.

In an online database, page images do not need to conform to the size restrictions found in a printed book. When converting these images back into a printed bound book, the page sizes are standardized in ways that maintain the detail of the original. For large images, such as fold-out maps, the original page image is split into two or more pages

Guidelines used to determine how to split the page image follows:

• Some images are split vertically; large images require vertical and horizontal splits.
• For horizontal splits, the content is split left to right.
• For vertical splits, the content is split from top to bottom.
• For both vertical and horizontal splits, the image is processed from top left to bottom right.

THE

VICTIM

OF

PREJUDICE.

VOL. I.

THE
VICTIM
OF
PREJUDICE.

IN TWO VOLUMES

By MARY HAYS,
AUTHOR OF
THE MEMOIRS OF EMMA COURTNEY

VOL I

Her Trumpet Slander rais'd on high,
And told the Tidings to the Sky,
Contempt discharg'd a living Dart,
A side-long Viper, to her Heart,
Reproach breath'd Poisons o'er her Face,
And soil'd and blasted ev'ry Grace,
Officious Shame, her Handmaid new,
Still turn'd the Mirror to her View,
While those, in Crimes the deepest dy'd,
Approach'd to whiten at her Side

Moore's Female Seducers

LONDON

PRINTED FOR J. JOHNSON, ST. PAUL's CHURCH-YARD.

1799.

ADVERTISEMENT

TO

THE READER.

IN a former publication, I endeavoured to inculcate an important leſſon, by exemplifying the errors of ſenſibility, or the pernicious conſequences of indulged paſſion, even in a mind of no common worth and powers. To avoid, as I conceived, the poſſibility of miſconſtruction, I ſpoke of my heroine, in the preface, not as an example, *but as a* warning : *yet the cry of ſlander was raiſed againſt me, I was accuſed of recommending thoſe exceſſes, of which I laboured to paint the diſaſtrous effects. Leſt dullneſs or malignity ſhould again wreſt my purpoſe, it may be neceſſary to premiſe, that, in deline-*

ating,

ating, in the following pages, the mischiefs which have ensued from the too-great stress laid on the reputation *for chastity in* woman, *no disrespect is intended to this most important branch of temperance, the cement, the support, and the bond, of social virtue: it is the* means only, *which are used to ensure it, that I presume to call in question.* Man *has hitherto been solicitous at once to indulge his own voluptuousness and to counteract its baneful tendencies · not less tragical than absurd have been the consequences! They may be traced in the corruption of our youth, in the dissoluteness which, like a flood, has overspread the land, in the sacrifice of hecatombs of victims.* Let man *revert to the source of these evils; let him be chaste himself, nor seek to reconcile contradictions.* —— *Can the streams run pure while the fountain is polluted?*

IN-

INTRODUCTION.

A CHILD of misfortune, a wretched outcaſt from my fellow-beings, driven with ignominy from ſocial intercourſe, cut off from human ſympathy, immured in the gloomy walls of a priſon, I ſpread my hands and lift my eyes to the Moral Governor of the Univerſe ! If, as I have been taught to believe, a Being exiſteth, who ſearcheth the heart, and judgeth not as man

VOL. I.　　　B　　　judgeth,

judgeth, to Him I make my laſt appeal from the injuſtice and barbarity of ſociety.

And thou, the victim of deſpotiſm, oppreſſion, or error, tenant of a dungeon, and ſucceſſor to its preſent devoted inhabitant, ſhould theſe ſheets fall into thy poſſeſſion, when the hand that wrote them moulders in the duſt, and the ſpirit that dictated ceaſes to throb with indignant agony, read; and, if civil refinements have not taught thy heart to reflect the ſentiment which cannot penetrate it, ſpare from the contemplation of thy own miſery one hour, and devote

devote it to the memory of a fellow-sufferer, who derives firmness from innocence, courage from despair; whose unconquerable spirit, bowed but not broken, seeks to beguile, by the retrospect of an unsullied life, the short interval, to which will succeed a welcome and never-ending repose.

THE

VICTIM of PREJUDICE.

CHAP. I.

IN the first dawnings of infant sensibility, the earliest recollections which I have of my being, I found myself healthful, sportive, happy, residing in a romantic village in the county of Monmouthshire, under the protection of Mr. Raymond, a sensible and benevolent man, a little advanced beyond the middle period of life, who, for some years past, had re-

B 3   treated

treated from the pursuits of a gay and various life, and, with the small remnant of an originally-moderate fortune, had secluded himself in a rural and philosophic retirement.

To the wisdom and kindness of my benefactor, who, with a contempt of vulgar prejudices, cherished notions somewhat singular respecting female accomplishments, I was indebted for a robust constitution, a cultivated understanding, and a vigorous intellect. I was early inured to habits of hardiness, to suffer, without shrinking, the changes and inclemencies of the seasons, to endure fatigue and occasional labour, to exercise my ingenuity and exert my faculties, arrange my thoughts and discipline my imagination. At ten years of age, I

could

could ride the foreft-horfes without bri-
dle or faddle; could leap a fence or fur-
mount a gate with admirable dexterity;
could climb the higheft trees, wreftle
with the children of the village, or min-
gle in the dance with grace and activity.
Tall, blooming, animated, my features
were regular, my complexion a rich
glowing brunette, my eyes vivacious and
fparkling, dark chefnut hair fhaded my
face, and floated over my fhoulders in
luxuriant profufion; my figure was light
and airy, my ftep firm, my afpect intelligent, and my mind inquifitive.

The modeft and candid reader will
excufe this feeming vanity in the defcrip-
tion of my perfonal accomplifhments,
when informed, that the graces, with
which nature had fo liberally endowed

B 4   me,

me, proved a material link in the chain of events, that led to the subfequent incidents of my life; a life embittered by unrelenting perfecution, and marked by undeferved calamities; the meafure of which appears at length to be filled up.

Mr. Raymond inftructed me in the rudiments of the French, Italian, and Latin, languages, in the elements of geometry, algebra, and arithmetic. I drew problems, calculated abftract quantities, and learned to apply my principles to aftronomy, and other branches of natural knowledge. The inftructions of my tutor were communicated with fo much kindnefs, my ftudies were fo blended with amufement, fo little reftraint was laid upon the freedom of my humour,

or

or the wild fimplicity of my age, that my leffons, my exercifes, and my fports, feemed but diverfified fources of pleafure and amufement.

Ignorant refpecting the authors or the circumftances of my birth, I felt too happy and too carelefs to make them fubjects of inquiry. Mr. Raymond, to my young and ardent imagination, appeared at once my parent, protector, and tutelar deity. I bounded into his arms after every fhort abfence; I knew no tranfport equal to that afforded me by his fmiles and careffes, and prattled to him without apprehenfion or difguife, I was unacquainted with fear, and comprehended neither the nature of, nor the temptations to, falfehood.

B 5 CHAP.

C H A P. II.

I Had scarcely completed my eleventh
year, when my benefactor was prevailed
upon, by the importunity of a friend, to
undertake the tuition of two youths, heirs
to a gentleman of an ancient family and
ample fortune; who, desirous of bestow-
ing upon them a liberal education, dreaded
to expose their morals to the contagion
of a great school.   Some embarrassments
of a pecuniary nature assisted in determi-
ning my patron, whose spirit had not always confined itself within the limits of
his income, to accede the more readily to
the proposal of his friend, and preparations
were made for the accommodation of
this addition to our little household.   E-
very

OF PREJUDICE. 11

very thing, which, at an early period of life, promiſes novelty, is attractive. Re-joicing in the anticipation of this acceſſion to our family, I waited impatiently for the hour that would bring me new aſſo-ciates in my ſtudies and companions in my ſports.

The wiſhed-for period at length ar-rived, when the Honourable Mr. Pel-ham, followed by his ſons, William and Edmund, alighted from a poſt-coach at the entrance of our rural habitation. Be-ing with Mr. Raymond in his ſtudy, on the introduction of our gueſts, I ſcrutinized with a lively curioſity their manners and appearance. Mr. Pelham ſeemed to be about the middle period of life, ſome years younger than my guardian, his carriage was ſtately and ſolemn, his air cold and

reſerved.

referved.   William, the elder of the
youths, was in his thirteenth year; tall,
well - proportioned, handfome, active,
bold, and fpirited.   Edmund, younger
by feveral years than his brother, was
fickly and delicate, his voice feeble, his
countenance amiable, and his manners
mild and gentle.

Some preliminary difcourfe enfued between Mr Raymond and his gueft, refpecting the abilities and future deftina-
tion of the lads, who were by no means
to degrade a long and illuftrious line of
anceftry by the practice of any profeffion
or commercial employment.   Mr. Pelham fummed up his directions, by adding
emphatically, that, above all things, it
muft be the care of the preceptor to
preferve his charge from forming any
impioper

improper acquaintance, or humiliating connections, which might tend to interfere with his views for their future dignity and advancement. The family-honour, he informed my patron, had been preserved uncontaminated for many generations, and it was his pride that it should descend unsullied to posterity.

The meaning of these expressions I by no means comprehended on their delivery, but various circumstances have since but too frequently recalled them to my recollection, and impressed them upon my feelings in characters never to be effaced. Mr. Pelham, during his stay, which was till the ensuing morning, scarcely honoured me with his notice, excepting by a slight inquiry if I was the daughter of his host.

" No,

" No, fir," replied my friend, " I
" have not the happinefs of calling this
" lovely girl mine, except by adoption.
" She is an unfortunate orphan, whom it
" is equally my duty and my delight to
" fhelter from a world that will hardly
" be inclined to do her juftice, and upon
" which fhe has few claims."

There was fomething in the tone of
Mr. Raymond's voice, while he thus expreffed himfelf, that thrilled through my
heart with a new and indefcribable fenfa-
tion. The awe with which I had been
impreffed by the prefence of his gueft
gave way to a more powerful and irrefiftible emotion, throwing my arms round
the neck of my benefactor, I burft into
tears, and fobbed upon his bofom. E-
qually

qually furprifed and affected by this
fudden tranfport, he gently foothed me;
while, to divert the paffion he had un-
warily excited, he propofed that I fhould
accompany the young gentlemen into
the garden, and fhew them our collection of botanical plants. For the firft
time in my life, I had been fenfible to
embarraffment, and a temporary feeling
of depreffion and apprehenfion; a pre-
lude, as it fhould feem, to thofe anxieties and forrows which have fince pur-
fued me with unmitigated feverity, a-
gainft which I have vainly ftruggled,
and whofe overwhelming confequences
I am no longer able to combat or e-
vade.

Withdrawing myfelf from the arms
of my patron, I breathed a heavy figh.
He

He kiffed the tear from my glowing
cheek, while his meek eyes beamed with
kindnefs.   I accepted his commiffion
with alacrity, pleafed to be delivered
from the prefence of Mr. Pelham, whofe
auftere manners chilled my fpirits, and
fufpended the light and joyous fenfations, which, till that inaufpicious moment, had converted every little incident of my life into a new fource of
pleafure and entertainment.   Relieved
from the conftraint impofed by the behaviour of his father, William, taking
my hand, and gazing in my face with
an expreffion of lively fympathy, addreffed me in kind and encouraging
accents.   We proceeded, followed by
his brother, to the garden, where the
impreffions from the preceding fcene
were quickly forgotten.   We laughed,
wreftled,

wreftled, romped, contended in various
fports and feats of activity, in the bold-
nefs and agility of which I emulated
my companion, while my daring fti-
mulated him to greater exertion. If I
found myfelf foiled by his fuperior ftrength
and ftature, yet, in courage, in fpirit, in dexterity, and refource, he was
compelled to acknowledge he had met
with no contemptible rival.

In a fhort time, from a mutual dif-
play of congenial qualities and an in-
terchange of kindnefs, we became tho-
roughly impreffed with affection for each
other. Enjoying the prefent, and anticipating the future, with the light and
fanguine fpirits of youth, I forgot, in
the fociety of the fon, the painful feelings infpired by the prefence of the father.

ther. Edmund, whom infirm health had,
by its enfeebling effects, prevented from
participating in our fports, feemed, neverthelefs, exhilarated by our gambols,
and caught, from fympathy, a portion
of the hilarity of which he was incapacitated from taking a more active
fhare.

CHAP.

CHAP. III.

A Generous emulation infpired me with redoubled ardour in the purfuit of my ftudies. William, with quick perceptions and a vigorous imagination, was carelefs, diffipated, fond of pleafure, and averfe to application: Edmund, with a mind and temperament lefs active and lively, outftripped, by habits more attentive and perfevering, the progrefs of his brother. While the gentle Edmund interefted my fympathy, and infpired me with tendernefs, the warm affections, lively feelings, and enterprifing fpirit, of William were better fuited to my habits and temper. In the hours of amufement, we became infeparable ; we

seemed

feemed animated but by one heart and
one mind; we took our leffons together; and, when (a cafe by no means
unfrequent) William loitered in his exercifes or left his tafk unfinifhed, I redoubled my diligence and application,
that I might have leifure to affift him.
Mr. Raymond perceived with pleafure
the harmony which fubfifted between us,
and encouraged us in reciprocal acts
of fympathy and kindnefs: regarding
youth as the proper feafon for the cul-
tivation of focial affections, he delighted
in obferving the guilelefs and innocent
teftimonies of friendfhip which we mutu-
ally manifefted and received. The difpofition of William was fomewhat im-
petuous, impatient of control, and li-
able to fudden gufts of paffion, yet
thefe emotions were tranfient; his impreffions,

preffions, more lively than permanent, readily yielded to new objects and new occurrences. An incident which occurred at this period, though in itfelf trifling, is too characteriftic to be omitted.

The lord of the manor, who refided not far from our cottage, was particularly curious in his fhrubs and fruit-trees, and we were ftrictly prohibited from trefpaffing, on any pretence or occafion, on his premifes. Sa4ntering, one fine fummer's evening, near the park-palings, we obferved, within the enclofure, but not far diftant, an open green-houfe, from the windows of which hung a large and tempting clufter of grapes, of uncommon ripenefs, bloom, and beauty.

" Mary,"

" Mary," faid William, taking my hand, and pointing to the forbidden fruit, " I have a great inclination to procure " fome of thofe grapes that hang fo " invitingly. What fay you? fhould " you not like, this warm evening, to " partake a refrefhment fo cooling and " delicious?"

" No, no, William," replied I, averting my eyes from the lufcious bait, " you " know my father," (fo was I accuf- tomed to call my dear benefactor,) " who never reftricts us unreafonably, " has, on this fubject, given us a par- " ticular caution."

" Mr. Raymond is over fcrupulous," rejoined William, reddening, and quick- ening

ening his pace. " And you," added he, leering flily in my face, " like the reft " of your weak fex, are timid and fpi- " ritlefs."

" Is this kind, William? Is it juft?"

" Well, but, Mary, I have a ftrange " fancy for thofe grapes. I wifh alfo " that you fhould fhare them with me. " Your father will know nothing about " the matter, unlefs we fhould be filly " enough to betray ourfelves."

" But fuppofe he fhould hear of it, " and queftion me on the fubject, I " never yet concealed any thing from " him ; and I could not tell a falfehood" (in a foftened voice) " even for *you,* " William."

" Foolifh

" Foolish girl! he loves you too well,
" and you know it, to be angry with
" you."

" Ah, William, is that a reason why
" I should venture to displease him?"

" Your friendship for me is weak,
" since you will hazard nothing to oblige
" me."

" But *you*, also, will incur his dis-
" pleasure, William."

" I care not; it is enough, I have
" given up the point. In future, I shall
" better know how to make an esti-
" mate of your courage and affection."

Saying

Saying which, he turned from me, apparently difgufted, and was prefently out of fight. I remained, for fome moments, involved in a train of reflections, equally painful and perplexing. The unkind and petulant reproaches of William had pierced my heart: he had alfo queftioned my courage. This I could have fubmitted to; but had he not likewife affected to doubt my *love?* — I paced backward and forward, agitated by contending feelings. Should I violate almoft the only injunction of my indulgent patron? Should I add to that violation the meannefs of concealment or evafion? My eyes filled with tears, and my bofom palpitated. Should I expofe myfelf to detection from the fquire and his family, and fuffer the

VOL. I. C imputation

imputation of gluttony and trefpafs?
An indignant glow fuffufed my cheek.
But, then, what a fweet compenfation
would the confcioufnefs afford, that it
was not for felfifh gratification I had
fubjected myfelf to hazard and cenfure,
but to ferve and oblige my friend. The
difficulties and poffible mortifications at-
tending the enterprife would but enhance
its value, I fhould prove, at once, my
fpirit and my affection: the rifk, too,
would be all mine, the abfence of William muft exonerate him from blame,
and his fhare in the tranfaction might
reft in my own bofom. to Edmund,
alfo, whom the fervour of the weather
has rendered feverifh and indifpofed,
how refrefhing and grateful would be
this delicious fruit The laft confideration fixed the wavering balance, and
confirmed

confirmed my refolution. To a young
cafuift thefe reafonings bore a fpecious
appearance: affuming the refpectable
forms of generofity and tendernefs, they
dazzled, and finally prevailed.

With fome difficulty, I furmounted
the fence, and proceeded boldly towards the green-houfe Having feized
and fecured the tempting bait, I was
about to retreat with the fpoil, when
a burft of mirth from behind a thicket,
accompanied with loud fhoutings, fufpended my fteps, and fixed me mo-
tionlefs with furprife. I held in my
hand the proof of my guilt, the confcioufnefs of which fhook my frame
with a trepidation to which it had been
little accuftomed. A tumultuous party
of young men iffued from a grove,

and advanced haſtily towards me: I attempted not to fly, but, rallying my ſpirits, firmly waited their approach.

" Ah! my little laſs," cried the foremoſt, ſeizing me, " have we caught " you in the fact? — Detection, upon " my ſoul!" (attempting to ſnatch the fruit, which I reſolutely graſped:) " a " true daughter of Eve!"

As I ſtruggled to diſengage myſelf from his hold, a large ſtraw hat, which ſhaded my face from the ſun, fell back, and, ſuſpended by the riband, hung upon my ſhoulders; over which, my diſhevelled hair ſtreamed in wild diſorder.

Starting

Starting backward a few paces, and ftaring rudely in my face, " By God!" faid he, " a little beauty! a Hebe! a " wood-nymph! I muft and will have " a kifs; and, d—n me! you fhall " be welcome to all the grapes in the " green-houfe."

Shocked and affrighted by a brutality of manner fo novel and unexpected, with a fudden fpring I evaded his grafp, and, winged by terror and difguft, flew towards the boundaries of the park with inconceivable fwiftnefs. Having diftanced my purfuers, and fcrambled over the fence, with my clothes torn, my hands and arms bruifed, fcratched, and ftreaming with blood, I rufhed towards the dear and well-

C 3　　　　known

known afylum, the peaceful manfion
of my revered benefactor, ftill retain-
ing in my hand the fatal caufe of my
fault and of my terror.   On the threfh-
old of our cottage I encountered Mr.
Raymond, accompanied by his pupils.
Panting, breathlefs, heated by the fervour of the weather, flufhed by the
confcioufnefs of guilt, and exhaufted by
perturbation and fatigue, I ran into his
arms, that feemed to open fpontaneoufly
to receive me.

" Mary! my child!' exclaimed my
more than father, in an accent of folicitude and alarm, " why this terror,
" this agitation?   What has injured,
" what has befallen, my child?"

Unable

Unable to reply, my head funk on my bofom, while a few tears, forcing their way, ftole down my burning cheek. Difengaging myfelf from the arms of my friend, I perceived William, whofe countenance manifefted evident figns of confufion, gliding from the prefence of his tutor, and ftealing gently into the houfe. I ftarted, and, precipitately advancing towards him, put into his hands the fruit I had fo dearly purchafed.

"What means all this?" interrogated Mr. Raymond. "Whence came thofe "grapes? Why do you give them to "William?"

C 4   "They

" They came, fir," (I dared not call
him by the endearing name of father,)
" from the green-houfe of Sir Peter
" Ofborne: I give them to William,
" becaufe —— *I love him.*"

William blufhed, and hung his head.

" Explain yourfelf, my child! You
" fpeak in enigmas."

" I have nothing more to fay, fir."

" Who gave you the fruit? and how
" know you that it belonged to Sir Pe-
" ter Ofborne?"

" No perfon gave it to me; I took it
" myfelf."

" How!

" How! what! took it yourfelf! is
" it poffible? How did you gain ac-
" cefs to the green-houfe ?"

" I climbed over the fence, and
" plucked the grapes, which hung from
" an open cafement."

Mr. Raymond appeared petrified with
aftonifhment.

" Who faw you? Whence came this
" blood? Who has wounded you and
" torn your clothes? How came you
" in this condition ?"

" I was difcovered by fome gentle-
" men, whom the trees had concealed
" from me. One of them feized and

C 5   " terrified

" terrified me: I efcaped from his
" hands, and, in my hafte to regain
" the road, bruifed and tore my-
" felf."

While I thus artleffly replied to the
inquiries of my friend, I ventured not
to lift my eyes to his: a confufed confcioufnefs of my fault flafhed upon my
mind, depriving it of its wonted confidence.

" Well, Mary," refumed he, and
fighed, " you have now only to give
" me a recital of the motives which
" influenced you to this extraordinary
" ftep, with the fame ingenuoufnefs with
" which you have already related the
" tranfaction and its confequences. I
" confefs, I know not how to fufpect
                                    " you

" you of gluttony : did you mean to eat
" thefe grapes ?"

" No, fir."

" Was it merely to prefent them to
" William that you fubjected yourfelf to a
" fituation thus painful and humiliating ?"

I blufhed, trembled, and was filent.

" Did William require of you this fa-
" crifice ?"

" No, fir."

" I perceive," replied he, coldly,
" you are not inclined to give me fa-
" tisfaction upon this fubject. I wifh
" not to *extort* your confidence."

My

My heart fwelled almoft to burfting; but I reftrained its emotions. I
fhed no teais; my downcaft eyes remained fixed upon the ground. Cold
fhiverings feized me, which were in a
few minutes fucceeded by a burning
heat. My lungs feemed oppreffed; a
pain darted through my temples; I re-
fpired with difficulty. Mr. Raymond,
coming towards me, took my hand:
the pulfe throbbed beneath his fin-
gers.

"Poor child!" faid he, in a tone
of concern, "you are in a high fe-
"ver; you have overheated your
"blood."

Leading

Leading me into the houſe, he delivered me to the care of the houſe-
keeper, who retired with me to my
chamber. I paſſed a reſtleſs night; and,
towards morning, became much worſe.
In the courſe of the enſuing day, the
ſymptoms appeared ſufficiently threatening to fill my benefactor with ſerious
apprehenſion, and induce him to call
in medical aid. The phyſician pronounced my diſorder to be a ſcarlet fever, which had lately been prevalent in
the neighbouring hamlet.

In the mean time, ſcarcely quitting
my apartment, Mr. Raymond watched
every turn of my diſeaſe, treating me
with the moſt ſoothing tenderneſs. This
kindneſs gave an additional pang to my
heart:

heart: I felt myself unworthy of his
goodnefs; and, by the ftruggles of my
mind, increafed the violence of my dif-
temper. On the third day, the fever
abated, and my diforder began to af-
fume a more favourable afpect. My
dear patron teftified the moft lively
joy, but I was ftill far from being re-
conciled to myfelf.

My young companions, I was informed, had, to preferve them from
infection, been removed to a neighbouring farm-houfe, and ftrictly inter-
dicted from approaching our habitation.

On the fifth day of my indifpo-
fition, while reclining on a fopha, in
a fmall room that looked towards the
garden,

garden, whither I had been removed for the benefit of the air, Mr. Raymond having juſt retired to his ſtudy, the door ſuddenly flew open, when William, ruſhing in, threw himſelf upon my neck, and, tenderly embracing me, burſt into a paſſion of tears.

" Ah, my dear Mary!" cried he, in a voice interrupted by ſobs, " I can " never pardon myſelf the ſufferings I " have occaſioned you. I was deter- " mined to ſee you and implore your " forgiveneſs, nor ſhould all the world " have prevented me."

As he thus ſpoke, my patron, alarmed at hearing an unuſual noiſe in the apartment, from which his ſtudy was not

far

far diftant, re-entered. I had difen-
gaged myfelf, with features expreffing
confternation and horror, from the embraces of William.

" Take him away!" exclaimed I,
clafping my hands together in an agony,
and trying to avoid him. " Oh, take
" him away! He will catch the fever;
" he will be fick and die; and, then,
" what will become of Mary!"

Mr. Raymond advanced with a ferious
and refolute afpect. William funk upon
his knees.

" Tell her, fir," faid he paffionately,
" that I have confeffed all the truth,
" that I repent of my folly and wicked-
" nefs, and fhall never be happy till
" I

" I have obtained her and your for-
" givenefs."

His tutor, without reply, led him
from the room; and, giving him in
chai.ge to a fervant, to be reconducted
to the farm, returned to me.

" What uneafinefs," faid he, on entering, " has this rafh boy occafioned
" us! I feaied to mention the fub-
" ject to my little girl," (tenderly taking my hands in his,) " left, in her
" weak ftate, it might have given her
" difturbance, but let me now affure
" her, that her conduct in the affair,
" though certainly imprudent and not
" entirely blamelefs, has neverthelefs
" endeared her to my heart with, if pof-
" fible, a thoufand additional ties."

I

I threw myfelf into his arms, and
wept aloud, delicious tears of reconcili-
ation and grateful affection: he wiped
them with his handkerchief, kiffed me
tenderly, and, artfully changing the fubject, gradually foothed and tranquillized
my fpirits.

C H A P.

C H A P. IV.

I Had scarcely recovered from the effects of my indisposition, when William, sickening, discovered evident signs of infection. Mr. Raymond, alarmed by these appearances, after having again removed Edmund, sent an express to Mr Pelham, with an account of the situation of his son. Mr. Pelham returned with the messenger. On his arrival, the eruption had appeared, attended with threatening symptoms. During many days, the event was doubtful: we fluctuated alternately between hope and fear. I could scarcely be torn from the apartment, to take necessary rest and refreshment: William would

receive

receive nothing but from my hands, while I wept inceffantly over fufferings I was unable to alleviate.

At length, the diforder took a favourable turn. William daily acquired health and ftrength, his father, every apprehenfion of danger being now removed, returned to town; and, in a few weeks, no other confequences remained of the malady than a flight degree of languor and weaknefs.

This incident, which I regarded as a grateful proof of his affection, added to the remembrance of his fufferings on my account, ferved but to endear him to me yet more tenderly. I redoubled my cares and efforts to oblige and amufe him.

As

As the health of William became entirely re-eftablifhed, we returned to our
fports and occupations with renewed fpirit and glee.

One fine autumnal morning, rambling
through the fields, juſt after fun-rife,
as was our cuftcm, we heard the cry
of the dogs and the fhouts of the hun-
ters. We ran, with youthful curiofity,
towards a lane, whence the mingled
founds, returned by the echoes, feemed
to proceed. We had fcarcely reached
the place, when a hare, panting, breathlefs, and limping, rufhed paft us; and
fell, a few paces diftant, to the ground.
I flew towards the diftreffed animal, and,
thoughtlefs of my danger, threw myfelf
befide it on the turf, endeavouring to
                                        fhelter

shelter it with my feeble arms. The dogs advanced in full cry; I shrieked, William ran to my assistance, when the huntsman, suddenly appearing in sight from a winding of the lane, and observing our perilous situation, called off the eager animals, who were within a short distance of their trembling, defenceless, prey. Some gentlemen riding up, one of them loudly cried to us to quit the hare, while the poor animal, his sides palpitating, seemed to look wistfully in my face, as imploring protection. My heart melted with compassion: I hovered still more closely over the panting victim, disdaining any reply to his savage persecutors. The gentleman, leaping from his horse, advanced towards me; when William, intercepting, dared to oppose him. Brandishing

diſhing his horſe-whip, he threatened
to exerciſe it upon my friend, when,
ſtarting from the ground, and ruſhing
between them, I received ſeveral ſmart
ſtrokes, deſigned for William, over my
neck and ſhoulders. The remainder of
the company now interpoſed.

" For ſhame, Sir Peter!" ſaid a gentleman, who, having alighted from his
horſe, haſtened to my relief: " do not
" exert this unmanly rage againſt de-
" fenceleſs children· the humanity, cou-
" rage, and ſpirit, of this little laſs de-
" ſerve better treatment."

" D—n me," replied the keen ſportſ-
man, " am I to have my ſport inter-
" rupted by a peaſant's brats?"

As

As his friend held his arm, perceiving William no longer in danger, I returned to my charge, who, exhaufted by fatigue, was unable to efcape from the fpot on which it had funk. My neck and arms bore marks of the rough difcipline I had received, yet I neither uttered a complaint nor fhed a tear: indignation infpired me with a fullen fortitude, while, in the fmart of blows acquired in the caufe of humanity and friendfhip, I found only a fource of triumph. The whole party, having by this time alighted, furrounded us, when my adverfary, after ftaring for fome moments rudely in my face, fhouted in a difcordant tone,

" May

" May I be d—ned if this is not
" the little thief that ftole the grapes
" from the green-houfe? By G—d!
" my pretty dear' you fhall not ef-
" cape me now; but fhall pay the
" full forfeit of all your trefpaffes."

Saying which, he feized me, and,
clafping me in his arms, kiffed me
with an odious violence. I fhrieked,
ftruggled, and fought, with all my
ftrength. William, feeing me fo freely
and roughly treated, fnatched the whip
of my perfecutor, which, in the con-
teft, had fallen to the ground, and af-
faulted him with fury. Obliged to relinquifh his prey, he turned to defend
himfelf from the attack of my cham-
pion, whom his companions, with dif-

ficulty,

ficulty, releafed from his vengeance. The gentleman who had at firft been my advocate again interpofed.

" I infift upon it, Sir Peter," faid he, in a refolute tone of voice, " that " you commit no more violence upon " thefe young people, who have given " you no ferious caufe of offence, and " whom I am determined to protect."

After fome altercation, peace was reftored, we were permitted to depart, and the hare was, by the general voice of the company, awarded to me, as a recompenfe for my courage and fufferings in its defence.

Mr. Raymond, to whom our unufual abfence had occafioned fome folicitude,

met

met us on our return. William related circumftantially to him all that had
paffed. Regarding me with looks of
affectionate concern and intereft, he ap-
plauded my fpirit and humanity, repeatedly preffing me to his heart. There
was an affecting folemnity in his voice
and manner that ftruck upon my fpirits. He fighed frequently, as he gazed
upon the marks which the difcipline of
the whip had inflicted, and turned from
me, as if to hide a ftarting tear.

" I do not mind them," faid I, obferving his concern. " Have you not
" taught me, my dear father, that, in
" the caufe of *right*, we fhould contemn
" bodily pain? Befides," (clafping my
hands together with an animated gef-
ture,) " I rejoice in thefe fcars, were

" they

" they not blows intercepted from Wil-
" liam?"

Mr. Raymond, apparently overcome
by an emotion that would no longer
be controlled, quitted us precipitately.

CHAP.

CHAP. V.

BY thefe little incidents, the innocent and growing tendernefs between myfelf and my youthful companion was increafed and cemented. For the firft time, reflections occurred to the mind of my benefactor that occafioned him fome uneafinefs: yet, he was too wife to rifk, by any premature hint or precaution, the giving a reality to what, at prefent, he hoped was but a chimerical evil.

The animal we had refcued from the fportfmen was, by our care and affiduities, in a fhort time reftored to health and vigour.

D 3

" Let

" Let us give him freedom," faid
I to William, who propofed to reftrain
him. " Liberty, my father has told
" me, is the trueft and moft invalua-
" ble good. He has no longer need
" of our affiftance : he would pine with
" us while fequeftered from his fellows
" and companions. let us not be more
" barbarous than the favages who would
" have fhed his blood."

To the juftice of thefe reafonings
William affented, and we reftored our
happy and bounding captive to his native woods.

Thefe incidents had impreffed me
with a horror for the name and character of Sir Peter Ofborne, whofe
grounds

grounds and their environs I cautiously avoided.

Happy in the society of my young companions, time glided swiftly away in a thousand varied pleasures. We continued to improve in stature and in knowledge: we received our lessons in common. The feeble health of Edmund was an impediment to his acquirements: William's gaiety and dissipation interrupted his application. I outstripped both my companions: with an active mind and an ardent curiosity, I conceived an enthusiastic love of science and literature. Mr. Raymond directed my attention, encouraged my emulation, and afforded me the most liberal assistance.

Mr.

Mr. Pelham occasionally recalled his
sons, to make short visits to his house
in London. During their absence, my
vivacity forsook me and my spirits lan-
guished. On their return, William and
I bounded into each other's embraces;
while, all life, spirit, and gaiety, we
laughed and prattled, eagerly related
the little occurrences of our separation,
and, in the joyous present and anticipated
future, forgot the anxieties and vexations
of the past.

William at length entered into his
nineteenth, and I into my seventeenth,
year. Tall, healthful, glowing, my per-
son already began to display all the
graces and the bloom of womanhood:
my understanding was cultivated and mature,

ture, but my heart fimple and guilelefs, my temper frank, and my manners wild and untutored. My benefactor had, for fome time paft, anxioufly
watched the growing attachment between myfelf and his pupil. He deeply
regretted the painful neceffity of check-
ing a fympathy at once fo natural, virtuous, and amiable. He knew not how
to debauch the fimplicity of my mind
by acquainting me with the manners
and maxims of the world. How could
he, to my unfophifticated underflanding,
explain the motives which influenced his
conduct? or, unfolding them, how be able
to repel my artlefs, but juft, reafoning?
Painful fufpicions affailed him: he began
to doubt whether, in cultivating my
mind, in foftering a virtuous fenfibility,
in imbuing my heart with principles of

juftice

juſtice and rectitude, he had not been betraying my happineſs! —— Gracious God! what muſt be the habits of society, which could give riſe to ſuch an apprehenſion? An apprehenſion, alas! which, in theſe embittered moments, I feel but too much inclined to believe verified. *Prudence* ſeems no longer to be underſtood in its juſt and original ſignification, — The wiſe government of our inordinate deſires, a graceful regard to the propriety of our actions, a rational and dignified ſelf-reſpect. in its ſtead has been ſubſtituted a ſordid calculation of ſelf-intereſt, a bigotted attachment to forms and ſemblances, a perſevering ſuppreſſion of every generous, every ardent, every amiable, affection, that ſhould threaten to interfere with our baſer and more ſiniſter views.

C H A P.

CHAP. VI.

ONE evening, after paffing the day with William in our ufual lively affectionate intercourfe, Mr. Raymond fent for me to his ftudy. I obeyed his fummons with alacrity, and, on entering, ran towards him with the lightnefs of fpirit with which I had been accuftomed to conform myfelf to his moft indifferent requefts. He appeared not to receive me with his ufual cheerfulnefs; an expreffion of perplexity fat upon his features, while a cloud hung over his brow. My fpirits caught the alarm.

" My

" My father!" said I, in an accent
of anxiety and concern, taking his hand,
and looking tenderly in his face; " you
" are not well. What has difcompofed
" you? Speak to me. Can I do no-
" thing to ferve or relieve you?"

" Sit down, my love! Nothing has
" happened: I am not ill, I merely
" wifh to have a little converfation with
" you."

" Ah!" kiffing his hands alternately,
" have I been fo unhappy as to dif-
" pleafe you? Do let me know my
" error, that I may inftantly repair it."

" You never difpleafed me, you are
" incapable of difpleafing me: I know
" of

" of no fault which you have, unlefs
" it be an excefs of goodnefs. The
" concern which I feel at prefent ari-
" fes folely from the fear that I fhall
" be compelled to wound the gentle
" nature of my beloved girl."

" Go on, dear fir; I am fatisfied,
" you cannot exact from me what is
" unreafonable, you cannot demand of
" me more than I will cheerfully per-
" form."

Clafping me to his breaft, he embraced me with paternal kindnefs. " I
" have been to blame to alarm you
" by this folemnity, there is no caufe
" for it," (and he affected to fmile;)
" your delicacy and your quicknefs will
" lead you readily to comprehend the
" motives

" motives which oblige me to require
" of you what may, at firſt, perhaps,
" appear a ſacrifice ſomewhat pain-
" ful."

I gazed on him with a mixture of
aſtoniſhment, curioſity, and ſolicitude.
He proceeded, after a few moments he-
ſitation.

" You are now, my dear Mary, ap-
" proaching towards womanhood: I be-
" hold the lovelineſs of your perſon and
" the graces of your mind with all a pa-
" rent's partial fondneſs, but with all a
" parent's anxiety.   Your own excellent
" underſtanding will ſuggeſt to you, that
" propriety of action varies at different
" periods of life; that our ſocial and
" relative duties are perpetually changing,
" and,

" and, as they change, fuggeft to us dif-
" tinct modes of conduct. The firft and
" moft earneft purpofe of my cares
" and precepts has been, by forming
" you to virtue, to fecure your *hap-*
" *pinefs:* for this *end,* I have laboured
" to awaken, excite, and ftrength-
" en, your mind. An enlightened in-
" tellect is the higheft of human en-
" dowments, it affords us an inex-
" hauftible fource of power, dignity,
" and enjoyment. ' Of extraordinary
" talents, like diamonds of uncommon
" magnitude, it has been truly faid,
" calculation cannot find the value.'*
" Their favoured poffeffors are the ge-
" nuine fovereigns of mankind: they

* *Holcroft's Anna St. Ives.*

" direct,

" direct, they model, they govern, the
" world. But I will not try to con-
" ceal from you, that the vivid fenfa-
" tions, exquifite fenfibilities, powerful
" energies, and imperious paffions, which
" neceffarily accompany fuperior men-
" tal excellence, have but too frequent-
" ly, when habits of felf-government
" and independence of mind have not
" been early and affiduoufly cultivated,
" ferved but to betray the poffeffor, to
" plunge him into deeper and more
" deplorable ruin, to gild the wreck
" over which humanity weeps and trem-
" bles. Poifons the moft deadly are
" produced amidft the luxurious vege-
" tation of the tropics: compared with
" the lion of the African defert, in
" ftrength, in fize, in ferocity, the fa-
" vage animal who inhabits the nor-
                              " thern

" thern wilderneſs is tame and power-
" leſs.

" I perceive, with pride and plea-
" ſure, the vigorous promiſe of your
" bloſſoming faculties, I rejoice that
" my efforts have not been fruitleſs,
" that my ſpeculations have not proved
" an idle theory, nor my plans and ex-
" pectations a philoſophic dream: yet
" the higheſt and the proudeſt boaſt of
" genius were vain, but as a *mean* to an
" *end*. If I have not ſecured your hap-
" pineſs and rendered you uſeful to ſo-
" ciety, if I have not taught you to
" ſubdue yourſelf, to ſubject your feel-
" ings, to direct your views ſteadily to
" objects worthy of your attention, to
" contemn the ſuggeſtions of a near and
" partial intereſt, to triumph over the
" imperious

" imperious demands of paſſion, to yield
" only to the dictates of right reaſon
" and truth; my cares have indeed been
" worthleſs and my efforts vain: in-
" finitely more enviable will be the lot
" of the peaſant, who, toiling ceaſeleſs
" through the day, draws from the ſte-
" rile earth a ſcanty ſuſtenance, ſatiſ-
" fies the cravings of nature, and re-
" poſes in the hovel of indigence;
" who has neither leiſure to feel, nor
" capacity to comprehend, the multi-
" plied ſources of anguiſh from which
" the ſhafts of diſappointment draw
" their deadly venom, while they tranſ-
" fix and rankle in the tender and ſuſ-
" ceptible heart."

My benefactor pauſed here: his face
glowed, his tones were unuſually touch-
ing,

ing, they thrilled through my nerves:
he looked wiftfully in my face: his eyes
were moift with tears, yet illumined
with a benign luftre; their mild and
penetrating rays feemed to pervade my
foul. Grafping his hand, I had funk
unconfcioufly upon my knees before him,
and, while I eagerly examined his features, caught every accent as it proceeded from his lips. My bofom throbbed refponfively to the fentiments which
he uttered: I held in my breath, left I
fhould interrupt or lofe a fingle fylla-
ble: I felt animated as by a divine en-
thufiafm, my thoughts elevated, my
mind expanded. For fome minutes after he ceafed to fpeak, I continued to
gaze, to liften; every faculty of my
foul abforbed, wrapt in attention. Raifing me from the ground, he gently
re-feated

re-feated me: I clafped my hands, and exclaimed with fervour,

"Name the facrifice you require, "diftruft not the mind you have form- "ed; your dictates and thofe of *rea-* "*fon* are the fame, they have ever been "uniform and invariable. Behold me, "my father, refigned to your will!"

Mr. Raymond rofe, vifibly affected, and traverfed the room with a quick, but unequal, pace. At length, turning towards me,

"It is I, my dear Mary," faid he, "who want firmnefs, who am unable "to give an example of the fortitude "I would fain inculcate. Your artlefs, "your affectionate eloquence unnerves "me.

" me. How fhall I tell you that I
" doubt I muft, for a time, rob my-
" felf of the joy of my life, the ten-
" der attentions, careffes, and fociety,
" of my little girl. Yes, it is, I feel,
" but too neceffary that we fhould fe-
" parate, for days, for months, perhaps
" for years."

I ftarted, trembled, fhuddered, I felt
a fudden revulfion of blood and fpirits;
in a moment my face was bathed in
tears. Seizing the hand of my benefactor, I wept bitterly.

" What have I done?" cried I paffionately, in a voice interrupted by fobs,
" that I muft be exiled from your pre-
" fence? Whom have I in the world
" but you and William? Ah! you will
" foon

" soon ceafe to be troubled with an
" unhappy orphan; I fhall not long
" furvive when banifhed from you!"

Yielding to the firft burft of feeling,
my patron folded me in his arms, and
fhed over me a flood of tears. His
manly fpirit for a time vainly contended with his emotions, till, making a
ftrenuous effort, he ftruggled with and
fubdued himfelf, affumed an afpect of
more compofure, and gently foothed
my diftrefs, till I became gradually refigned and tranquil.

" It is from *William*," refumed Mr.
Raymond, in a feverer tone, " that I
" think it prudent to feparate you."
A convulfive tremor fhook my frame. —
without feeming to remark my emotion,
he

he proceeded.   " I will not deceive
" you, my child, by falfe and feeble
" pretences.   With the purity and the
" fimplicity of your heart I am well
" acquainted.   The mutual harmony
" and tendernefs which has fubfifted
" between you and your young com-
" panions I have hitherto regarded with
" equal approbation and pleafure, but
" the feafon now approaches when, even
" by the excefs of a laudable and vir-
" tuous fenfibility, you may be be-
" trayed into a fituation the moft threat-
" ening and perilous.   You are now
" no longer children, you are too lovely
" and too fufceptible to indulge in an
" intercourfe, however amiable, inno-
" cent, and full of chaims, which may
" lead to confequences that timely cau-
" tion only can avert.   Were it not
                                " for

" for certain prejudices, which the world
" has agreed to refpect and to ob-
" ferve, I fhould perceive your grow-
" ing tendernefs with delight, and hail
" it as the prefage and the fecurity of
" virtue; but I am refponfible to ano-
" ther tribunal than that of *reafon* and
" my own heart for the fentiments and
" conduct of this young man, and I
" dare not betray my truft. Your child-
" ifh affociation has been a reciprocal
" fource of moral and mental improve-
" ment: thus far let us congratulate
" ourfelves, and reap the benefit: but
" the imperious ufages of fociety, with
" a ftern voice, now command us to
" paufe. Her mandates, often irratio
" nal, are, neverthelefs, always defpotic:
" contemn them, — the hazard is cer-
" tain, and the penalty may be tremen-
                                    " dous.

" dous. Some vigorous minds dare to
" encounter thefe perils: doubtlefs, we
" are indebted to them: they help to
" fhake the fantaftic fabric: but woe be
" to thofe who, in this arduous con-
" teft, mifcalculate their powers! I con-
" fefs, I wifh not to fee the name of
" my girl enrolled in the tragic lift ei-
" ther of martyrs or of victims: foli-
" citous for her *happinefs*, I would have
" prudence temper her heroifm. Need
" I enlarge? Muft I add — *You can*
" *never be the wife of William Pel-*
" *ham?*"

A fhock of electricity appeared to
rend my quivering nerves; my colour
changed, my bofom palpitated, a faint
ficknefs feemed for an inftant to ftop
the current of my blood; the next

VOL. I. E moment

moment it rushed impetuously through my veins, distended my heart, and dyed my face and neck with crimson. After a short pause, he proceeded.

" His father has far other views for
" him, views, in which, at a future
" period, he will probably acquiesce.
" Yes, the guileless, generous, ardent,
" youth, brought up in rural shades,
" on his entrance into society, will, by
" irresistible contagion and insensible gra-
" dations, become *a man of the world.*
" 'Let him be preserved from humi-
" liating connections,' said Mr. Pelham,
" when he entrusted him to my charge.
" In the opinion of those who class
" with the higher ranks of society,
" poverty, obscure birth, and the want
" of splendid connections, are the only
                    " circumstances

" circumstances by which he can be
" degraded. The beauty, the virtue,
" the talents, of my child, in the eye
" of philosophy, are an invaluable dow-
" ry; but philosophers are not yet the
" legislators of mankind. William is
" destined for the theatre of the world;
" he will imbibe the contagion of a
" distempered civilization. *Mary must*
" *not be contemned by the man she loves.*"

My friend ceased to speak, while he
pressed my hands in his, and, bending
fondly over me, watched every turn of
my varying countenance. His impres-
sive manner, the interesting subject of
his discourse, had commanded all my
attention: a flood of ideas gushed upon
my mind, novel, affecting, terrible, and
bewildered my disordered senses. Ac-

E 2   customed

cuftomed to love William from my
childhood, to receive and to return his
innocent and lively careffes, I had not
inquired into the nature of my senfations,
and I now underftood them but obfcurely.

Mr. Raymond's difcourfe had conveyed to me no diftinct idea, till "*You*
"*can never be the wife of William Pel-*
"*ham*," repeated emphatically, founded
in my ftartled ears, in which it ftill
continued to vibrate. Many of the fentiments and reflections of my patron
ftruck me as at once new, extraordinary, and inconfiftent. My ideas were
confufed, my reafoning powers fufpended: undefined apprehenfions and fufpicions arofe in my mind; my principles
were unhinged and my paffions thrown
into

into diforder. Mr. Raymond perceived
the conflict, the contending feelings,
which fhook my fluctuating fpirits.

" Retire, my beloved girl," faid he
tenderly, " for the night, try to com-
" pofe yourfelf, and reflect on what
" has paffed at your leifure. God for-
" bid that I fhould tyrannize over your
" heart: to your own judgement I en-
" truft your conduct. Confide in me
" with franknefs, I may advife, but I
" will ufe no control. You are wholly
" free, your actions unwatched and un-
" reftrained: I abide your determina-
" tion."

I threw myfelf into his arms; I regarded him, in filence, with a difturbed
and mournful air: he folded me to his

E 3   bofom,

bofom, led me to the entrance of my chamber, and quitted me precipitately.

Unhappy parent! unhappy tutor! forced into contradictions that diftort and belie thy wifeft precepts, that undermine and defeat thy moft fagacious purpofes! — While the practice of the world oppofes the principles of the fage, education is a fallacious effort, morals an empty theory, and fentiment a delufive dream.

CHAP.

C H A P. VII.

I PASSED the night in a tempeft of contending paffions: I fought to arrange my thoughts and tranquillize my feelings in vain. Mr. Raymond's difcourfe had awakened in my heart new defires and new terrors, to which, till that moment, it had been a ftranger. The novelty of my fenfations at once furprifed and alarmed .me : happy in the prefent and thoughtlefs of the future, I had neither dreaded danger nor anticipated viciffitude. If nature had yet fpoken in my heart, fo foft and gentle were her whifpers, that her voice had hitherto been unheeded. The caution of my patron appeared to have given a

E 4 fudden

sudden and premature existence to the
sentiment against which he sought to
arm me. Acquainted with the human
mind, of this effect he was but too well
aware; yet, in the critical circumstances
in which he found himself, he perceived no other alternative; but, while
tenderly sympathizing in the pain he
conceived himself compelled to inflict,
he confided firmly in the principles he
had implanted.

Towards morning, exhausted by perturbation, I sunk into slumber, nor a-
woke till the day was far advanced.
The bright beams of the sun, darting
through my curtains, restored me to
sense and recollection, and, for the first
time in my life, I awoke to anguish.
Springing from the bed, I dressed in
                              haste,

hafte, when a trampling of horfes' feet under my window attracted my attention. Haftily opening the cafement, I difcovered feveral gentlemen on horfe-back, attended by fervants, in the midft of whom were William and Edmund.

The eyes of William were turned anxioufly towards my apartment, when, perceiving me, he uttered a fhout of joy, and, throwing himfelf from his horfe, flew back to the houfe. Trembling, though I knew not why, I defcended haftily the ftairs, and met him on the landing-place.

" I am going," faid he, " my dear " Mary," catching me in his arms, and tenderly embracing me, " a fhort tour " with fome friends of my father's,

E 5   " and

" and propofe to be abfent fome days.
" So idle were you this morning, that
" I began to fear I muft quit you
" without faying *farewel!* and taking a
" parting kifs."

Mr. Raymond approached: my colour changed, my tremor increafed, the
careffes of William, no longer received
and returned with artlefs joy, dyed my
cheeks with fcarlet, poured through my
veins a fubtle poifon, and fhook my
trembling frame. Precipitately difengaging myfelf from his embraces, a
fervant at the fame inftant haftily fum-
moning him to join his party, I returned to my chamber with faultering
fteps. Unconfcioufly, I regained the
window: William, as he mounted, waved
his hand to me, repeating the action
with

with his face turned as he rode forwards. Straining my fight to look after him, when the winding of the road concealed him from my view, I burst into a flood of tears. " O God!" exclaimed I, clasping my hands passionately, and raising my streaming eyes, " he is gone! " I have seen him, perhaps, for the " last time! Why must we be torn " asunder? Why can *I never be the* " *wife of William Pelham?* What ty- " ranny is this? When reason, virtue, " nature, sanctify its emotions, why " should the heart be controlled? who " will dare to control it?" — I wept anew, sobbed audibly, my bosom bursting with grief. For the first time in my life, I was ready to accuse my guardian of in-justice and caprice. It was many hours ere I reasoned myself into more composure.

I remained in my chamber during the greater part of the day. My pation satisfied himself with sending up refreshments and kind inquiries, but made no effort either to see or to converse with me.

In the evening, I sought him in the garden, whither he was accuftomed, in mild weather, to repair. Perceiving my approach, he advanced towards me with features expreffing kindnefs and sympathy.

" I am prepared," faid I, in a firm tone, my face averted, " to conform " myself to your commands."

" *Commands,*

" *Commands*, Mary! I am no ty-
" rant, I am unaccustomed to com-
" mand."

" Pardon me, sir, I am sensible of
" your goodness, but I dare not de-
" ceive you. When you tell me that
" the affection I have hitherto delighted
" to cherish for your pupil is become
" dangerous and improper; that cer-
" tain prejudices, with the nature of
" which I am unacquainted, rend us
" asunder, and convert what was in-
" nocent and laudable into I know
" not what of pernicious and crimi-
" nal; that tremendous judgements and
" penalties threaten us, from which there
" is neither appeal nor escape; I confess
" I comprehend nothing of all this which
" you

" you have not deigned to unravel:
" neverthelefs, my confidence in your
" wifdom and kindnefs impel me to
" refign myfelf to your guidance, and
" to truft, that time and experience
" will gradually difentangle my appre-
" henfions, and unfold to me what now
" appears wholly inexplicable."

" Yes, my child! this, at prefent,
" I own, is a fubject too fubtle for
" reafoning; *time and experience* only
" can evince the propriety of my con-
" duct. I fhould confound with reluc-
" tance, by factitious diftinctions, the
" rectitude of your judgement, or blaft,
" by worldly maxims, the ingenuous
" virtues of your expanding mind.
" Convinced of your fincerity, and a-
" ware of your fortitude, I accept the
" facrifice

" facrifice you offer; but, while I talk
" your heart and your courage, be af-
" fured, that, by the trueft, the ten-
" dereft, fympathy, mine is perva-
" ded."

" Yet do not mifconceive me, my
" father; with my prefent views and
" feelings, I dare not engage to love
" William no longer. I pretend to
" no heroifm, though, aware of my
" inexperience, I yield, for the prefent,
" my conduct to your directions. Mark
" out for me the path I fhould pur-
" fue; my heart affures me that you
" have not exacted from me this firft
" inftance of *implicit refignation* without
" important reafons, reafons that you
" will not always think it juft to with-
" hold."

Mr.

Mr. Raymond appeared greatly affected, and fighed deeply. " Mary,"
faid he, in a folemn and plaintive accent, " you have fulfilled my expec-
" tations, you have fmoothed the dif-
" ficulty of inftruction ; a difficulty,
" alas ! of which I have been but too
" well aware. Human life has not
" unaptly been compared to a warfare:
" whether rendered fo by nature or by
" civil inftitution, it is for future ex-
" periments to determine : for the pre-
" fent, we have too frequently but a
" choice of evils ; in which cafe, to
" felect the lighteft is all that bene-
" volence can advife or wifdom per-
" form. What was in my power, the
" pleafures of childhood, I have la-
" boured to fecure to you unalloyed.
                                    " In

" " In a wild and uncertain calculation
" of the future, the happinefs of the
" *prefent* (all that properly can be termed
" our own) ought not to be trifled
" with : yet there are limits, even upon
" this principle, that to overleap would
" become infanity; the prefent crifis,
" if I miftake not, marks the boun-
" dary, and imperioufly calls upon me
" to difpenfe with the rule to which I
" have hitherto facredly adheied,—That
" of impofing no penalty on a being
" capable of reafon, without ftrictly de-
" fining the motives by which I am
" actuated."

" It is enough, fir, tell me where
" and to whom I fhall go; I confent
" to be banifhed from all that gives
" to life its charm; I confide, without
                    " fhrinking,

" shrinking, in your judgement and af-
" fection."

" I have a friend," resumed Mr. Raymond, after a pause, " a respectable and
" worthy man, who resides on the sea-
" coast, about fifty miles from hence,
" on a curacy of sixty pounds a year.
" He is a man of sense and letters,
" his wife an accomplished amiable wo-
" man. By contracting their wants,
" they contrive to be happy and in-
" dependent on a scanty stipend. My
" girl, during the period which I think
" it necessary to deprive myself of her
" society, will, I have no doubt, find,
" under the humble roof of this excel-
" lent pair, a cordial welcome and a
" hospitable asylum. In the bosom of
" virtue and domestic peace, her mind
                              " will

" will quickly regain its wonted fere-
" nity. Contemplating the artlefs pic-
" ture of nature in one of her rareft
" and moft favoured lots, her heart
" will expand in delightful fympathy,
" and, in the fimple joys which fur-
" round her, quickly lofe fight of thofe
" overweening confiderations which, at
" prefent, fo entirely abforb it."

" Let us go, my father," feizing
his hand, and fpeaking rapidly, " let
" us go this moment, ere new trials,
" before which my ftrength may melt
" away, incapacitate me for fulfilling
" the arduous duties which my mifgi-
" ving heart already but too forcibly
" forebodes."

" I underſtand you, my child, and
" I reſpect your reſolution; yet for-
" get not that, amidſt the viciſſitudes
" and the calamities of life, a firm and
" an independent mind is an invaluable
" treaſure and a never-failing ſupport.
" The canker moſt pernicious to every
" virtue is *dependence*, and the moſt fatal
" ſpecies of bondage is ſubjection to the
" demands of our own imperious paſ-
" ſions. Retire, and court the repoſe
" of which your pale cheek and lan-
" guid eyes but too plainly indicate your
" need, and to-morrow early we will
" prepare for the execution of our pro-
" ject."

My dear benefactor embracing me tenderly, I returned to my chamber. To
the

the conflict which had lately shaken my soul, a gloomy tranquillity succeeded; the still whispers of a self-approving heart sustained me; while resting with grateful love and implicit truth, as on omnipotent truth and goodness, in the cares and tenderness of my friend, hope undefined and indistinct consolation stole upon my spirits, and gradually lulled them in balmy repose.

CHAP.

C H A P.　VIII.

I AROSE with the dawn, and bufied myfelf in preparations for my departure, repelling, with folicitude, every recollection that might enfeeble my fpirits or unnerve my refolution. I repeated to myfelf inceffantly, " Has not " my kind patron juft and irrefiftible " claims upon the mind which, with " unremitting affiduity, he has laboured " to form ? Dare I to difappoint his " hopes and difgrace his precepts in " the moment of trial, the moment " which decides the fuccefs of his cares? " Have I not, in the whole of his " paft conduct, at once confiderate, " wife, and good, a foundation for my " truft?

" truſt? Does he ſternly call upon me
" to ſubmit to authority? Is it to his
" own paſſions he requires the ſacri-
" fice of mine? Does he aſſume the
" vindictive tone of an infallible judge,
" from whoſe deciſions there remains
" no appeal? Does he, with ſtoic pride,
" inſult the ſenſibilities for which nature
" has incapacitated his heart, or which
" time and experience have combined
" to chill? Does he mock the feel-
" ings, does he contemn the weakneſs,
" which his firmer mind repels? Ah,
" no! it is not the auſtere parent, the
" tutor, the patron, who, preſuming on
" his claims, derides the tenderneſs and
" the ardour of youth, no, it is the
" friend, gentle, candid, benignant, con-
" temning every privilege, diſdaining all
" ſubterfuge, uſing no deception, who,
" while

" while conſtrained to wound the heart
" through which he has been wont to
" diffuſe gladneſs, weeps in tender ſym-
" pathy, who, while he confeſſes re-
" ſerve, and laments its neceſſity, ap-
" peals to the rectitude of his paſt con-
" duct, appeals to the kindneſs to which
" every action, every expreſſion, eve-
" ry feature, bear irreſiſtible teſtimony.
" Nor ſhall he appeal in vain · a confi-
" dence thus generous I dare not be-
" tray. Far be from my heart, then,
" theſe weak and womaniſh regrets: to
" a determined ſpirit, to ſuffer is not
" difficult; but the vice of ingratitude
" ſhall never taint my ſoul."

A generous heroiſm nerved my mind,
throbbed in my boſom, glowed on my
cheek, a ſpirit congenial to artleſs youth,
by

by whom the veil of fociety, behind which corruption and contradiction lurk, has not been rent. My eyes regained their luftre, and my features their wonted fpirit.

On the firft fummons, I joined Mr. Raymond at the breakfaft-table : he read, in the ferenity, the triumph, of my countenance, the victory I had gained. How fweet, how grateful, were his approving fmiles! I enjoyed them as an earneft of future conquefts, as a reward to which my heart proudly whifpered its claim.

A chaife drew up to the door, into which, followed by my benefactor, I lightly fprang. Stifling a figh, and feizing the reins, I quickly left behind the fcene of all my pleafures, while peace fpread its halcyon wings, and fled for ever.

Every fubfequent incident of an e-ventful life has but led the way to new perfecutions and new forrows, a-gainft which the pureft intentions, the moft unconquerable fortitude, the moft fpotlefs innocence, have availed me no-thing. Entangled in a feries of un-avoidable circumftances, hemmed in by infuperable obftacles, overwhelmed by a torrent of refiftlefs prejudice, wearied with oppofition, and exhaufted by con-flict, I yield, at length, to a deftiny againft which precautions and ftruggles have been alike fruitlefs.

CHAP.

CHAP. IX.

IT was late in the evening when we drew near the place of our destination. Alighting at a small neat house, in the cottage-style, with barns and out-houses adjoining, we were met, on our entrance, by its respectable owner, who, on recognizing Mr. Raymond, uttered an exclamation of mingled joy and surprise.

" To what fortunate accident," said he, in a tone of animation, cordially greeting his friend, " am I indebted for " this unexpected pleasure?"

F 2 " I

" I have a charge," replied my guardian, " a precious charge, which, for " a short period, I would willingly consign to the protection of my worthy " friends, because there is none in whom " I have equal confidence."

As he ceased speaking, we entered, conducted by our host, a small parlour, in the simple furniture of which, and ornamental drawings uniformly arranged against an oaken wainscot, an air of taste was manifest. Mrs. Neville, the wife of the curate, was seated near a casement, shaded, on the outside, by the luxuriant foliage of a spreading vine, through which the twilight dimly gleamed. Two children, blooming as cherubs, played at her feet: she held a book

book in her hand half-clofed, over which
fhe feemed to mufe. On our entrance,
ftarting from her pofition, and throwing afide the author who had engaged
her attention, fhe advanced haftily towards us, teftifying, on the appearance
of Mr. Raymond, a lively joy. Some
minutes paft in mutual inquiries and con-
gratulations.

" Behold," faid my benefactor, taking my hand, and prefenting me to
his friends, " behold the dear child in
" whofe praifes my heart has fo often
" overflowed with all a parent's paitial
" fondnefs! I am conftrained, for a
" time, to bereave myfelf of her pre-
" fence: do I prefume too far on your
" friendfhip when I flatter myfelf that,
" beneath your hofpitable roof, I may,

F 3   " for

" for a while, fecure to her a welcome
" afylum ?"

With a conciliating grace, this amiable pair frankly accepted the proffered
truft, quickly re-affuring, by a polifhed
urbanity of manners, my doubting fpi-
iits. Lights being brought and refrefh-
ments fet before us by a ruftic maiden,
paft times and occurrences became the
fubjects of converfation in this little circle of friends, during which I had leifure to contemplate more minutely the
manners and lineaments of my hofts.
Mr. Neville appeared to be between
five-and-thirty and forty years of age:
his figure was tall and commanding,
his complexion florid: dark brown hair
unfoiled by powder, and parting on his
forehead, contrafted its whitenefs: his
                              afpect

aspect was somewhat severe, bold, and manly, yet tempered by benignity, repelling assumption rather than inspiring dread: his manners were cheerful, his temper apparently equal, his conversation intelligent, bespeaking a mind alike conversant with men and books: his sentiments occasionally assumed a higher tone, discovering a latent ardour and an activity of mind for which his present situation afforded insufficient scope; but a momentary recollection seemed to check these feelings, and restore to his temper its habitual serenity. The appearance of Mrs. Neville, who was somewhat younger than her husband, indicated a delicacy of original texture rather than an infirm state of health. Her complexion was olive, inclining to pale, yet varying with ex-

F 4 ercise

ercife or fentiment, when a charming
flufh would crimfon her cheek: her
eyes were dark, mild, and penetrating,
yet fufceptible of fpirit when kindled
by paffion or fentiment: her countenance, without pretenfion to beauty, had
in it an expreffion full of fenfe and
foul: there was a fafcination in her
fmile; and her flexible voice, when
modulated by tendernefs, took the affections captive: an emphatic propriety marked her pronunciation, her mind
feemed ftored with knowledge, though
of a varied and defultory nature, her
imagination elevated, and not wholly
untinctured with romantic views and
feelings: her manners were habitually
ferious, an exceffive fenfibility at times
even gave them the appearance of melancholy, but, exquifitely fenfible to focial

cial pleafure, in the prefence of thofe whom her heart acknowledged, fhe became animated and fprightly: the predominant paffion of her foul, teftified in every action, every expreffion, every glance, was, an enthufiaftic love for her hufband, a love at once ineffably tender, chafte, and dignified: her children were little lefs the objects of her tender folicitude.

It was not poffible for a heart like mine to contemplate this interefting family without a lively prepoffeffion: I anticipated the pleafure of cultivating their friendfhip and expanding my fenfations. Involuntarily I repeated to myfelf, " Why cannot I, with fweet ma-" gic, draw into one circle all I revere " and love? Why cannot I increafe

F 5 " and

" and multiply, a million-fold, thefe
" delightful fympathies? — My heart,
" with inexpreffible yearnings, continu-
" ally prompts me to unite, to bind,
" myfelf to my fellow-beings by every
" focial and relative tie."

On retiring for the night, I was conducted by Mrs. Neville to a fmall neat
chamber, where, after renewing her af-
furances of friendly welcome, and kindly
foothing my agitated fpirits, fhe left me
to my repofe.   Mr. Raymond, having
refifted the folicitations of his friends for
a longer refidence under their hofpitable roof, had fignified his intention
of departing early in the enfuing morning.   I rofe with the fun, and haftened
to his apartment.   My dear benefactor,
little lefs affected than myfelf by our

firft

firſt mournful ſeparation, folded me to his boſom, and, while I wept in his arms, mingled his tears with mine.

" Your tenderneſs, my ſweet girl," ſaid he, " pierces my heart; your ſen-
" ſibility unmans me. I have, per-
" haps, been wrong: God knows, I
" would not inflict on your gentle na-
" ture one unneceſſary pang: even now,
" if you requeſt it, you ſhall return
" with me. I impoſe no fetters, I
" will truſt to the rectitude of your
" feelings."

" No, my friend, my father," replied I, in a voice half-ſtifled with e-
motion: " forgive my weakneſs: my
" confidence in you is unbounded, but
" nature will, for a time, aſſert her

F 6 " powerful

" powerful rights. You have juft claims
" upon my fortitude, upon my affec-
" tion. Go! leave me! You will not,
" you cannot, forget your child!"

I ftruggled with my feelings, and
fuppreffed my tears. I dared not pronounce the name of *William*, a name
engraven on my heart, a name for ever
on my lips. My patron read in my
eyes the law which I impofed on myfelf: he preffed my hand, fighed, a-
verted his face. Once more tenderly
embracing me, he precipitately quitted
the room, accompanied by our hoft,
who, entering at the fame inftant, had
invited him to partake of a refrefhment prepared by Mrs. Neville, and informed him that the chaife was in readi-
nefs.

I returned to my chamber, where I remained till fummoned to the break-faft-table. I had, during the interval, reafoned myfelf into more compofure, and, rejoining my friends with affumed cheerfulnefs, fought to banifh from my heart every enervating remembrance, e-very defponding feeling.

In a few days, my mind appeared to have recovered, as with an elaftic force, from the fudden fhock it had fuftained, and to have refumed its habitual cheer-fulnefs. I fought occupation, and af-fifted Mrs. Neville in her domeftic e-conomy and in the management of her dairy. By admirable order, attention, and dexterity, this amiable pair, upon an annual income of fixty pounds, con-trived

trived to preferve even an air of li-
berality. It is true, the product of a
well-planted garden, and the profits of
a few acres of land, cultivated by the
labour of the worthy curate, added fomething to their yearly ftore. The morning, lengthened by early rifing, was devoted to bufinefs, in which equal fkill
and perfeverance were difplayed. In
the after-part of the day, literature, mufic, the inftruction of their children, a
ramble among the neighbouring ham-
lets, (to the fick and infirm inhabi-
tants of which they were beneficent
friends,) a walk on the fea-beach,
through the meadows, or on the downs,
divided their time. Not an hour paffed
unimproved or vacant: when confined
by inclement feafons to their tranquil
home, Mrs. Neville employed herfelf
with

with her needle in preparing simple vest-
ments for her houshold, while her hufband read aloud selected paffages from
a small collection of books, which was
annually increafed by an appropriated
fum. Mufic frequently concluded the
evening: Mrs. Neville touched the pi-
ano-forte with more feeling than fkill,
and accompanied by her voice (fweet,
but without compafs) simple canzo-
nets, impaffioned airs, or plaintive bal-
lads.

Through this happy family, perfect
harmony and tendernefs reigned: Mr.
Neville loved and entirely confided in
his wife, of whofe value he was juftly
fenfible; while her affection for him had
in it I know not what of tender folicitude, of exquifite foftnefs, of ardent
devotion,

devotion, which, to hearts lefs fufceptible, would appear exceffive or inconceivable. Their children, lovely and
promifing, were equally their delight
and care: they formed, between their
parents, a new and a more facred bond:
their expanding faculties and budding
graces authorized and juftified a parent's fondeft hopes. *Happinefs*, coy
and fair fugitive, who fhunneft the gau-
dy pageants of courts and cities, the
crowded haunts of vanity, the reftlefs
cares of ambition, the infatiable purfuits
of avarice, the revels of voluptuoufnefs,
and the riot of giddy mirth, who turneft
alike from faftidious refinement and brutal
ignorance, if, indeed, thou art not a phantom that mockeft our refearch, thou art
only to be found in the real folid pleafures
of nature and focial affection.

CHAP.

CHAP. X.

IN the bosom of this charming retirement, several weeks glided away in tranquillity. I received frequent letters from my guardian, which spoke of his pupils, but in general terms. The health of Edmund, he informed me, appeared to decline daily · a warmer climate had been advised by his physicians, in consequence of which, Mr. Pelham appeared inclined to send his sons on a continental tour, but that nothing was yet determined upon.

A train of painful reflections revived in my mind on this intelligence: how could I daily behold the tender and rational

tional

tional felicity of the interesting family in which I resided, and preserve my heart from drawing painful comparisons? How could I suppress secret murmurs at the factitious scruples to which I seemed a victim? Torn from my lover, he had, perhaps, disgusted with my inexplicable conduct, resigned and forgotten me. He wrote not, he came not: " Al-
" ready," I sighed to myself, " he is
" become *a man of the world!* He
" doubtless acquiesces, without reluc-
" tance, in those senseless prejudices to
" which I have tamely submitted, whose
" nature I am utterly unable to com-
" prehend." My mind became disquieted, my spirits lost their tone, disgust seized upon me, my wonted amusements were tasteless, I avoided the society of my friends, their mutual endearments

pierced

pierced my foul, and filled my eyes with tears. I fought folitude, and funk into gloomy rêveries.

Wandering one evening alone upon the beach, I feated myfelf on a jutting part of a rock, overhanging the fea: the air was ferene, the breeze fighed foftly, the waves, flowly fucceeding each other, broke on the fhore, and the furf dafhed at my feet: every object was in unifon with my feelings. As I contemplated the expanfe of waters which flowed around me, a mournful folemnity ftole over my fpirits: abforbed in thought, the tide, which was rifing, infenfibly gained upon me, and it was not till my retreat was cut off that I obferved myfelf encompaffed by the waves, and became confcious to the pe-

iils.

rils of my fituation. — My feet were already wet, and the fpray of the fea dafhed over me. I ftarted with an involuntary emotion of terror, and, cafting my eyes round for fuccour, thought I perceived at a diftance, through the obfcurity of the twilight, an object white, but indiftinct, which, on its nearer approach, I difcovered with joy to be a fail. I waved my handkerchief, as a fignal of diftrefs, and uttered a loud cry. The boat at length drew near, appearing to contain a party of gentlemen, who hailed me as it advanced. I continued to wave my handkerchief, and, in a few minutes, was extricated from my danger, and lifted by one of the gentlemen into the veffel.

" By

" By G—d, my pretty maid," faid my deliverer, obferving my garments wet, " you were in a critical fitua- " tion, and have had a fortunate ef- " cape."

A fhuddering feized me on recogni- zing the voice of Sir Peter Ofborne. Since the adventure of the chafe, I had feen him occafionally pafs the houfe of Mr. Raymond, to whom he had made fome overtures towards an acquaintance, which my patron had uniformly eva- ded. I had once or twice met him in my rambles, but had always fled from him, and, till this moment, had avoided a direct rencontre. I drew my hat over my face, and, fhrinking from his bold eyes, accepted, without reply,

a

a feat which was offered me. My filence being imputed to the effects of
my late apprehenfions, the gentlemen
preffed me to take refrefhment, which,
bowing, I rejected with a motion of
my hand. The odious Ofborne, who
appeared to be inebriated, was not to
be thus repulfed : feating himfelf befide me, and peering under my hat,
he encircled my waift with his left arm,
while, with his right hand, he feized
mine. Struggling to difengage myfelf,

" I prefume, gentlemen," faid I, with
fpirit, " you do not conceive yourfelves
" entitled, by the relief you have ac-
" cidentally afforded me, a relief which
" gives me a double claim upon your
" honour and humanity, to treat me
" with infult."

" Faith!"

" Faith!" exclaimed my perfecutor, " it is fo; I fufpected it from the very firft " glance; it is my fair fugitive herfelf."

" Yes, fir," replied I, with increafed vivacity, " I am, indeed, the young " woman who has been, more than " once, a fufferer from your brutality. " I infift upon being releafed this mo- " ment. I do not expect from you the " manners of a gentleman, but I will not " be intimidated or conftrained."

The wretch feemed ftruck with a temporary awe by my refolute and fpirited manner. His companions interfering, he was perfuaded, though not without imprecations and reluctance, to relinquifh his feat.

We

We landed in safety, and, escorted
by the whole party, who would not be
prevailed upon to leave me, I repaired
to the cottage of my friends.   Mr.
Neville, having been alarmed by my
unusual absence and the lateness of the
hour, had but just returned from an anx-
ious and fruitless search.   I was welcomed
by my amiable hosts with unaffected
joy, when my conductors, having received polite and fervent acknowledge-
ments for their timely interposition, departed.

Early in the ensuing morning, a ser-
vant, in a gay livery, arrived, with a
billet of inquiry, from Sir Peter, after
my rest and health; to which was added an apology for his behaviour of
the

the preceding evening, and an entreaty to be allowed to pay his respects to me. To this epistle I returned a brief and cold answer, thanking him for the service he had been instrumental in rendering me, and declining the proposed visit.

In the vicinity of the village in which I at present resided, was a town of fashionable resort, for the benefit of sea-bathing; the season for which being now at its height, sufficiently accounted for the late incident.

My repulses served but to stimulate my tormentor: he beset my paths, haunted me daily, and overwhelmed me with adulation and offensive gallantry. His understanding, though not of the

higheft order, was by no means contemptible, but his manners were pro-
fligate and prefuming; they alike pro-
voked my indignation and difguft. I at
length determined, during his ftay in
the country, to confine myfelf wholly to
the houfe: but neither did this avail
me; he forced himfelf upon Mr. Neville with an undaunted effrontery, breaking in upon our employments and re-
creations, till my friend, juftly incenfed,
refolved to fubmit no longer to an in-
trufion thus unfeafonable and imperti-
nent. Upon his next vifit, he fignified to him in firm, but temperate,
language, that his company was un-
welcome, that it was an interruption to
the occupations of the family, that it
was offenfive to his gueft, and that he
muft beg leave, in future, to decline
an

an acquaintance equally unwished-for and unfuitable.

This plain and manly remonftrance, though impatiently received and haughtily refented, neverthelefs produced its effect: yet, on quitting the houfe, the infolent man of fafhion menaced my hoft, in obfcure terms, with future retribution. Tender fears were, by this incident, awakened in the breaft of Mrs. Neville for the fafety of her beloved hufband; but, in a few days, to our mutual relief, we were informed that our adverfary had actually quitted that part of the country.

G 2 CHAP.

CHAP. XI.

SOME weeks after thefe tranfactions, my friends being from home, on a vifit of humanity, fitting one evening alone in my apartment, indulging in a melancholy retrofpect, I was roufed from my rêverie by the entrance of the fervant-girl, who haftily informed me that a fine young gentleman, (a ftranger,) on horfeback, had that moment arrived, that, having alighted and inquired for Mifs Raymond, fhe had conducted him into the parlour, where he waited with feeming impatience to fpeak to me. I changed colour; a flattering conjecture darted through my mind, while an univerfal tremor feized my limbs. With

a

a throbbing heart and faultering fteps, I repaired to the parlour, and, the next inftant, found myfelf in the arms of William. It was fome time before either of us acquired fufficient compofure for articulate expreffion; our joy was exceffive and tumultuous; we mingled tears with our mutual embraces. My lover overwhelmed me with broken and tender reproaches for having quitted him fo abruptly, for having fo long left him uncertain of my fituation.

"Alas!" replied I, "did you know "what I have fuffered ——" I hefitated: my heart was rent by contending paffions; confufed notions of danger and impropriety, of refpect for the judgement of my guardian, ftruggled with my native fincerity: I trembled; I felt

the

the blood alternately forſake and ruſh
back to my heart, which a faint ſickneſs
overſpread.   I ſunk into a chair, and remained ſilent.

" I underſtand you," ſaid William, regarding me with a paſſionate and mournful air, " but too well : you are a vic-
" tim to control, you have tamely ſub-
" mitted to a tyranny that your heart
" diſavows; your wonted ſpirit and firm-
" neſs are ſubdued."

" Hold!" reſumed I, " be not un-
" juſt ! Mr. Raymond, in the ſacrifice
" which he requires of us, is guided by
" conſiderations the moſt diſintereſted.
" he impoſes nothing, he appeals to my
" reaſon and affections, and his claims
" are reſiſtleſs.   I underſtand not, I con-
                                    " feſs,

" fefs, the extent of the motives which
" influence him, but affuredly his paft
" conduct entitles him to my truft."—
I proceeded to relate what had paffed
between my patron and myfelf previous
to our departure. — " I knew not,"
added I, in a low accent, with downcaft eyes and an averted face, " that
" the regard I felt for you differed, in
" any refpect, from our mutual and
" infantine fondnefs, till Mr. Raymond
" awakened my fears, and alarmed my
" tendernefs, by telling me that I muft
" feparate myfelf from you, that ' I
" muft never be the wife of William
" Pelham,' that he would become *a*
" *man of the world,* and contemn my
" artlefs affection."

G 4   " It

" It is falfe," replied William with vehemence, who had liftened to my recital with evident indignation and impatience, " it is falfe as hell! *I love* " *you,* Mary, and will never receive " any other wife. Mr. Raymond does " my father injuftice: it is true, he is " the flave of honour, but he is not " fordid: an alliance with your guardian, a man of education and a gentleman, to whom, no doubt, you are " connected by ties of blood, will do " our family no difcredit, and *love* will " make us happy, though our fortunes " fhould be moderate."

My lover proceeded to paint his paffion with all the eloquence of ardent, youthful, feeling. He informed me, that,

that, after my departure, he had funk
into fadnefs; that he knew not, till then,
the excefs of his affection for me; that
his tutor had, for fome time, evaded his
inquiries, but, at length, overcome by
his importunity, had named to him the
place of my prefent abode, at the fame
time recapitulating and enforcing the motives of his conduct. " Immediately,"
added he, " I procured a horfe, and,
" without fpeaking of my intentions,
" early the next morning took the road
" to this place, where I have but now
" arrived."

The return of Mr. and Mrs. Neville,
to whom I introduced my friend as a
pupil of Mr. Raymond, put a period
to our difcourfe. They preffed him,
during his ftay in the country, to ac-

G 5   cept

cept an apartment at their houfe, a requeft to which he acceded with vifible
fatisfaction.   Racking inquietude difturbed my mind, as various paffions bewildered my judgement and affailed my
heart.   I difcerned not on which fide
lay the path of duty : my reafon became
weakened by contradictory principles.
Thus, the moment the dictates of virtue,
direct, and fimple, are perplexed by
falfe fcruples and artificial diftinctions,
the mind becomes entangled in an in-
extricable labyrinth, to which there is
no clue, and whence there is no efcape.

, I threw myfelf on my bed, at the
hour of retirement, vainly feeking to col-
lect and arrange my fcattered thoughts:
fleep fled from my eye-lids; I arofe,
and,

and, feizing a pen, addreffed my benefactor.

I acquainted him with the arrival of
his pupil; I endeavoured to paint to
him my emotions, I befought his aid;
I expoftulated with him refpecting the
tafk he had impofed upon me; I reproached him for the conflict to which
he had expofed me; I regretted the
placid days of my childhood; and confeffed I underftood but obfcurely the
caufes of the change which I experienced. — " I am not weak," faid I,
" neither will I be the flave of my
" paffions. *I love William Pelham*, but
" am ready to renounce him the moment
" my reafon is convinced that virtue de-
" mands the facrifice."

Having

Having thus poured out my spirit, I became more tranquil. A few hours slumber refreshed my wearied faculties, yet the morning found me dejected and languid.

William, charmed with the interesting manners and family of his hosts, spoke with rapture of their mutual tenderness. "How poor, how contemptible," said he, "are fortune's most lavish gifts! "Why, my sweet girl, should we suf- "fer the prejudices of others to enslave "us? Let us purchase a cottage, and "hide ourselves from the world, su- "premely blest in each other. What "can be added to the felicity of mutual "love?"

I fighed involuntarily. " Yes, my
" friend, I doubt not that fuch are
" your prefent feelings. While my own
" heart beats with refponfive fympa-
" thies, I know not why I fhould dif-
" truft their continuance; yet how can
" I efface from that mifgiving heart the
" fearful prefage that even yet vibrates
" on my ftartled ear, —— ' Mary will
" be contemned by the man fhe loves;
" William Pelham will become *a man of*
" *the world' ?*"

" Cruel and unjuft girl! how have I
" merited fufpicions thus injurious?"

Ah! how full of charms, how infi-
dious, is the eloquence of a beloved
object! While my love pictured to my
imagination,

imagination, in glowing colours, the pleasures of an union which nature, reason,
and virtue, should combine to render
perfect, my heart melted within me,
I caught the ineffable sympathy, the
injunctions of my patron faded from
before me, I became animated, as it
were, with new powers, with a new existence, time seemed doubled by a lively
and exquisite consciousness to every in-
stant as it passed, yet, undefinable contradiction! I regretted its rapid flight,
and panted to eternize the fleeting moments. — " We loved each other; we
" beheld only our mutual perfections:
" in the midst of our transports, we
" mingled our tears, tears purer than
" the dew of heaven, delicious tears,
" creating the most exquisite rapture.
" We were in that bewitching deli-
                                    " rium

" rium which rendered even the con-
" ftraint we impofed upon ourfelves an
" honourable facrifice that added a zeft
" to our happinefs."*

---

* *Rouffeau Emille.*

CHAP.

CHAP. XII.

FROM thefe enchanting vifions I was at length roufed by a packet from my guardian. Retiring to my apartment, I unfolded it with emotion.

" My child," faid this revered friend, " your prefent circumftances wring from " my heart a narrative that will wound " your gentle nature; a narrative which " it was my purpofe for ever to have " withheld from you. I yield, with " anguifh, to the neceffity and to the " perils of your fituation.

" You have hitherto remained igno-
" rant of the authors of your birth,
" I

" I ſtudied to ſupply to you paternal
" duties; it was my care that nothing
" ſhould remind you of their loſs. I
" ſucceeded: all your hours were mark-
" ed with active enjoyment. I culti-
" vated your faculties and exerciſed your
" affections: I left you no time for lan-
" guor or retroſpect. Aware of the
" diſadvantages which might, too pro-
" bably, attend your progreſs in life,
" I ſought what was in my power, to
" ſecure to you without alloy the hap-
" pineſs of the preſent: yet it was my
" arduous purpoſe, while promoting your
" enjoyment, to render even your plea-
" ſures ſubſervient to a higher view,
" — That of invigorating your frame and
" fortifying your ſpirit, that you might
" be prepared to meet the future, to
" ſuffer its trials, and brave its viciſſi-
" tudes,

" tudes, with courage and dignity. I
" perceive, with felf-gratulation, the fruit
" of my labours, I fee in you all that
" my moft fanguine wifhes prefaged.
" I know you equal to encounter, to be
" victorious, in the conflict that awaits
" you; a conflict in which my affec-
" tion and prudence can no longer avail
" you.   But, while anticipating your
" victory, believe me not unmindful of
" your fufferings: while I perceive in
" them the feeds of future ftrength and
" energy, my coward heart and fofter-
" ing arms yearn to fhelter the child
" of my bofom from the gathering
" ftorm. I proceed to ftate to you
" thofe particulars of your birth, which,
" in your prefent circumftances, become
" too important to juftify a longer con-
" cealment.

                              " The

" The younger brother of a refpec-
" table family, at the age of one-and-
" twenty, with a liberal education and
" a fmall fortune, I became mafter of
" myfelf and of my actions. I paffed
" fome years in the diffipations cufto-
" mary to young men of my age and
" rank: at length, wearied with a heart-
" lefs intercourfe, while my fortune
" daily diminifhed, I determined to feek,
" from the intereft of my numerous ac-
" quaintance, fome lucrative office; to
" marry, and cultivate domeftic endear-
" ments. In thefe difpofitions, I faw,
" and became enamoured of, a young
" woman, amiable and accomplifhed,
" the idol of fond, but weak, parents,
" who had lavifhed, on the adornment
" of this darling, for whofe advance-

" ment

" ment they had formed ambitious pro-
" jects, fums which their fortunes were
" little able to fuftain. I frankly, though
" fomewhat indifcreetly, offered to the
" lovely Mary, whom Nature had form-
" ed in her moft perfect mould, my
" hand and my heart. Rejecting my
" addrefs with expreffions of refpect,
" fhe ingenuoufly acknowledged that her
" heart had already furrendered itfelf;
" yet, with an engaging air, fhe foli-
" cited my friendfhip; modeftly add-
" ing, that, affected by the prompti-
" tude and generofity of my propo-
" fals, it would be her pride to be
" deemed worthy of my efteem.

" I continued occafionally to fee her:
" I watched in vain for my rival, with
" the jealous eye of love: an air of
" myftery

" myſtery ſeemed to hang over the af-
" fair, which I was utterly unable to
" penetrate. My fair friend became
" reſtleſs and diſquieted; languor over-
" ſpread her fine features, internal agi-
" tation preyed upon her ſpirits, her
" temper grew unequal, her bloom fa-
" ded, and her health appeared daily
" to decline. I perceived the ſtruggles
" of her mind; I perceived that a ſe-
" cret malady devoured her: I ſought
" her confidence, with a determination
" of ſerving her, to the ſacrifice of my
" own feelings; but all my inquiries
" were uniformly evaded. Finding our
" intercourſe uſeleſs to her, and deſtruc-
" tive of my own peace, I began to
" meditate its diſſolution. An offer
" occurred of accompanying a young
" man, a college-friend, on a foreign
" tour.

" tour. Eagerly availing myself of this
" opportunity, I agreed to an immediate
" departure, expecting that change of
" objects, time, and absence, would
" produce on my mind their usual ef-
" fects.

" At the expiration of five years, I
" returned to my native land: a series
" of diffipation had almost effaced from
" my heart the traces of its former
" impreffions, till they were painfully
" renewed by a cataftrophe full of hor-
" ror. Returning, one evening, at a
" late hour, with a party of friends,
" from a convivial meeting, our ears
" were affailed, as we paffed a tavern
" of doubtful reputation, with a tumul-
" tuous noife, in which, amidft fhouts
" and imprecations, the fhrieks of wo-
" men

" men and the cries of murder, min-
" gled with the clashing of swords,
" might plainly be distinguished. Rush-
" ing towards the apartment from whence
" the alarm appeared to proceed, we
" perceived, amidst a promiscuous group
" of people, a gentleman extended on
" the floor, bathed in blood, who ap-
" peared to be expiring. Beside him
" stood a man, with a fierce and gloomy
" aspect, forcibly detained by the spec-
" tators, from whom he struggled to
" free himself. A woman, with a wan
" and haggard countenance, her clothes
" rent and her hair dishevelled, had
" fainted in the arms of a ruffian who
" supported her.

" ' Secure them,' exclaimed the mas-
" ter of the hotel, to a constable who
" entered

" entered with the watch; ' thofe are the
" murderers!'

" It was fome time before we could
" learn the particulars of this terrible
" fcene that prefented itfelf to us, which,
" we were at length informed, had ori-
" ginated in a brutal and licentious con-
" tention for the favours of the unhappy
" wretch who had fainted, and who
" was accufed of holding, while his an-
" tagonift ftabbed him, the arm of the
" dying man.

" In the midft of the tumult, my
" eyes involuntarily returned every mo-
" ment to the features of the miferable
" caufe of this cataftrophe: the remains
" of uncommon beauty might ftill be
" traced in a form and countenance
" ftained

" ftained with blood, difordered by re-
" cent inebriation, disfigured by vice,
" and worn by difeafe. A confufed re-
" collection bewildered my thoughts,
" and gave to my heart a quicker im-
" pulfe. As, abforbed in reflection, I con-
" tinued to gaze upon her, fhe breathed
" a heavy figh, and, raifing her languid
" eye-lids, her eyes, wild and vacant, en-
" countered mine. by degrees, their ex-
" preffion became more fixed and re-
" collected; fhe appeared eagerly to ex-
" amine my features; a flufh overfpread
" her livid countenance, fucceeded by
" a death-like palenefs Starting from
" the arms of the perfon who fupported
" her, and clafping her hands with con-
" vulfive energy, in a tone piercing and
" tremulous, fhe pronounced my name,
" and, uttering a deep groan, fell in a

Vol. I.   H   " fit

" fit at my feet. The found of her
" voice thrilled through my foul; my
' ideas fucceeded to each other with the
" rapidity of lightning, while my heart
" inftantly recognized, in a fituation
" thus tremendous and degrading, the
" idol of its youthful affections, the
" lovely, unfortunate, felf abandoned,
" Mary! ———— Great God! what, in
" that terrible moment, were my emo-
" tions! —— The blood poured in a tide
" towards my brain, hollow founds rang
" in my ears, the lights danced before
" my dazzled fight, every object be-
" came indiftinct: I ftaggered fome
" paces backward, while palpable dark-
" nefs appeared to envelope me. —— Re-
" turning to recollection, I gazed round
" me in vain for the phantom which
" feemed to have unfettled my reafon.
                                " The

" The room was cleared, a waiter and
" one of my companions only remain-
" ing: thefe were chafing my hands and
" temples with vinegar, and affiduoufly
" bufying themfelves in promoting my
" recovery.

" In reply to my incoherent and fran-
" tic inquiries, I learned that the wound-
" ed man had expired, the weapon, on
" examination, being found to have pe-
" netrated his lungs, that the mur-
" derer, with the wretched woman his
" accomplice, had been conveyed to
" prifon, the latter apparently infenfi-
" ble.

" On the fucceeding morning, in a
" ftate of inconceivable anguifh, I re-
" paired to the gaol. I knew not how

H 2 " to

" to inquire for the wretched victim
" of senfuality and vice by a name en-
" thufiaftically treafured in my memory;
" a name affociated with every tender,
" every melting, recollection; a name
" held by my imagination facred and
" unfullied, a name, which, till the laft
" fatal evening, to pronounce without
" reverence I fhould have confidered as
" profanation!   I ftarted and fhuddered
" as the gaoler abruptly founded it in
" my ears.   I put into his hand a piece
" of gold, in return for which he brought
" me a flip of paper, blotted and fcarcely
" legible, in which, with difficulty, I de-
" ciphered the following words: —

" 'To Mr. Raymond.

" 'I knew you; and, by my emo-
" tion, betrayed myfelf to you.   There
                              " wanted

" wanted but this to fill up the mea-
" fure of my fhame. I am about to
" expiate my crimes: feek not to avert
" my fate. In furviving virtue and
" fame, I have already lived but too
" long. I yearn for death: fhould I
" find it not in the juftice of my coun-
" try, my own arm fhall effect my
" deliverance. I owe to you a hif-
" tory of my difgrace: expect it, if
" my heart-ftrings burft not previoufly
" afunder. My dying-requeft will ac-
" company the infamous tale. In the
" mean time, make no effort to fee
" me — unlefs the man, whofe invaluable
" heart I once contemned, feeks to glut
" his vengeance by beholding me ex-
" pire at his feet! — Return! Difturb
" not my remnant of life! We meet
" no more! " ' MARY.'

H 3 " I

" I regained my apartments : a gush
" of tears relieved my boiling brain; I
" wept with infantine tenderneſs. Se-
" cluding myſelf from ſociety, I waited,
" in dreadful ſuſpenſe, the iſſue of theſe
" cruel tranſactions.

" Some weeks elapſed. The trial
" of the unhappy culprit drew near.
" Conſidering her prohibition as the que-
" rulous language of deſpair, I ſtrained
" every nerve, I left no effort untried,
" to ſoften the evidence of her guilt,
" to avert or to mitigate her ſentence.
" My endeavours were fruitleſs. con-
" demnation was pronounced, and re-
" ceived with triumph rather than with
" ſubmiſſion. I ſought to procure a
" parting-interview. my ſolicitations were
                              " uniformly

" uniformly and steadily rejected. The
" fatal morning now arrived when the
" woman on whom my soul had once
" fondly doated, whom yet, in her fall-
" en state, my heart yearned to snatch
" from the cruel destiny which awaited
" her, forfeited her life on a scaffold,
" by the hands of the executioner, to
" the sanguinary and avenging laws of
" her country.

" My child! I would have spared
" both you and myself this terrible re-
" cital. The wounds of my heart, thus
" rudely torn open, bleed afresh. I
" hasten, from the soul-sickening re-
" collection, to the developement of
" what yet nearer imports you. Read,
" in the enclosed packet, the memo-

H 4   " rial

" rial conveyed to my hand the day
" subsequent to this deplorable cataf-
" trophe.

" 'To Mr. Raymond.

" 'How far shall I go back? From
" what period shall I date the source
" of those calamities which have, at
" length, overwhelmed me?—Educated
" in the lap of indolence, enervated by
" pernicious indulgence, foftered in ar-
" tificial refinements, misled by specious,
" but false, expectations, softened into
" imbecility, pampered in luxury, and
" dazzled by a frivolous ambition, at
" the age of eighteen, I rejected the
" manly addrefs and honeft ardour of
" the man whose reafon would have
" enlightened, whose affection would
" have supported me, through whom
                                    " I

" I might have enjoyed the endearing
" relations, and fulfilled the respecta-
" ble duties, of mistress, wife, and mo-
" ther, and listened to the insidious
" flatteries of a being, raised by fashion
" and fortune to a rank seducing to
" my vain imagination, in the splen-
" dour of which my weak judgement
" was dazzled and my virtue overpow-
" ered.

" 'He spoke of tenderness and ho-
" nour, (prostituted names!) while his
" actions gave the lie to his preten-
" sions. He affected concealment, and
" imposed on my understanding by so-
" phistical pretences Unaccustomed to
" reason, too weak for principle, cre-
" dulous from inexperience, a stranger
" to the corrupt habits of society, I
H 5   " yielded

" yielded to the mingled intoxication
" of my vanity and my senses, quit-
" ted the paternal roof, and resigned
" myself to my triumphant seducer.

" ' Months revolved in a round of
" varied pleasures: reflection was stun-
" ned in the giddy whirl. I awoke not
" from my delirium, till, on an un-
" founded, affected, pretence of jea-
" lousy, under which satiety veiled it-
" self, I found myself suddenly deserted,
" driven with opprobrium from the
" house of my *destroyer*, thrown friend-
" less and destitute upon the world,
" branded with infamy, and a wretched
" outcast from social life. To fill up
" the measure of my distress, a little
" time convinced me that I was about
" to become a mother. The money
                                    " which

" which remained from my profuse
" habits was nearly exhausted. In the
" prospect of immediate distress, I ad-
" dressed myself to the author of my
" woes. Relating my situation, I im-
" plored his justice and his mercy. I
" fought in vain to awaken his ten-
" derness, to touch his callous heart.
" To my humble supplications no an-
" swer was vouchsafed. Despair, for
" awhile, with its benumbing power,
" seized upon my heart!

" ' Awaking to new anguish, and re-
" calling my scattered faculties, I re-
" membered the softness and the ease
" of my childhood, the doating fondness
" of my weak, but indulgent, parents.
" I resolved to address them, resolved
" to pour out before them the confes-

H 6   " sion

" fion of my errors, of my griefs,
" and of my contrition. My lowly
" folicitations drew upon me bitter re-
" ·proaches: I was treated as an aban-
" doned wretch, whom it would be
" criminal to relieve and hopelefs to at-
" tempt to reclaim.

    " ' At this crifis, I was fought out
" and difcovered by a friend (if friend-
" fhip can endure the bond of vice)
" of my deftroyer; the man who, to
" gratify his fenfuality, had entailed,
" on an unoffending being, *a being who*
" *loved him*, mifery and certain perdition.
" My declining virtue, which yet ftrug-
" gled to retrieve itfelf, was now affailed
" by affected fympathy, by imprecations
" on the wretch who had deferted me,
" and an offer of afylum and protection.
                " ' My

" " My heart, though too weak for
" principle, was not yet wholly cor-
" rupted: the modeſt habits of female
" youth were ſtill far from being ob-
" literated; I ſuſpected the views of the
" guileful deceiver, and contemned them
" with horror and juſt indignation. Chan-
" ging his manners, this Proteus aſſumed
" a new form, prophaned the names
" of humanity, friendſhip, virtue; gra-
" dually inſpiring me with confidence.
" Unable to labour, aſhamed to ſoli-
" cit charity, helpleſs, pennyleſs, fee-
" ble, delicate, thrown out with re-
" proach from ſociety, borne down with
" a conſciouſneſs of irretrievable error,
" expoſed to inſult, to want, to contu-
" mely, to every ſpecies of aggrava-
" ted diſtreſs, in a ſituation requiring
                                    " ſympathy,

" sympathy, tenderness, assistance, ——
" From whence was I to draw fortitude to
" combat these accumulated evils ? By
" what magical power or supernatural
" aid was a being, rendered, by all
" the previous habits of life and educa-
" tion, systematically weak and helpless,
" at once to assume a courage thus da-
" ring and heroic ?

" ' I received, as the tribute of hu-
" manity and friendship, that assistance,
" without which I had not the means
" of existence, and was delivered, in
" due time, of a lovely female infant.
" While bedewing it with my tears,
" (delicious tears ! tears that shed a
" balm into my lacerated spirit !) I
" forgot for awhile its barbarous fa-
" ther, the world's scorn, and my blast-
" ed

" ed profpects: the fenfations of the
" injured woman, of the infulted wife,
" were abforbed for a time in the
" ftronger fympathies of the delighted
" mother.

" My new friend, to whofe tender
" cares I feemed indebted for the fweet
" emotions which now engroffed my
" heart, appeared entitled to my grate-
" ful efteem : my confidence in him
" became every hour more unbounded.
" It was long ere he ftripped off the
" mafk fo fuccefsfully affumed ; when,
" too late, I found myfelf betrayed, and
" became, a fecond time, the victim
" of my fimplicity and the inhuman
" arts of a practifed deceiver, who
" had concerted with the companion of
" his licentious revels, wearied with his
                              " conqueft,

" conqueſt, the ſnare into which I fell
" a too-credulous prey.

" 'Evil communication, habits of vo-
" luptuous extravagance, deſpair of re-
" trieving a blaſted fame, gradually ſti-
" fled the declining ſtruggles of virtue,
" while the libertine manners of thoſe,
" of whom I was now compelled to be
" the aſſociate, rapidly advanced the
" corruption ;

    " 'Took off the roſe
  " ' From the fair forehead of an innocent love,
  " ' And plac'd a bliſter there.

" ' In a mind unfortified by princi-
" ple, modeſty is a bloſſom fragile as
" lovely. Every hour, whirled in a
" giddy round of diſſipation, ſunk me
" deeper in ſhameleſs vice. The mo-
     " ther

" ther became ftifled in my heart : my
" vifits to my infant, which I had been
" reluctantly prevailed upon to place
" with a hireling, were lefs and lefs
" frequent. Its innocence contrafted
" my guilt, it revived too powerfully
" in my heart the remembrance of what
" I was, the reflection on what I might
" have been, and the terrible convic-
" tion, which I dared not dwell upon,
" of the fate which yet menaced me.
" I abftained from this foul-harrowing
" indulgence, and the ruin of my mind
" became complete.

" ' Why fhould I dwell upon, why
" enter into, a difgufting detail of the
" gradations of thoughtlefs folly, guilt,
" and infamy ? Why fhould I ftain
" the youthful purity of my unfortu-
" nate

" nate offspring, into whose hands these
" sheets may hereafter fall, with the
" delineation of scenes remembered with
" soul-sickening abhorrence? Let it
" suffice to say, that, by enlarging the
" circle of my observation, though in
" the bosom of depravity, my under-
" standing became enlightened: I per-
" ceived myself the victim of the in-
" justice, of the prejudice, of society,
" which, by opposing to my return to
" virtue almost insuperable barriers, had
" plunged me into irremediable ruin.
" I grew sullen, desperate, hardened.
" I felt a malignant joy in retaliating
" upon mankind a part of the evils
" which I sustained. My mind be-
" came fiend-like, revelling in destruc-
" tion, glorying in its shame. Aban-
" doned to excessive and brutal li-
          " centiousness

" centiousness, I drowned returning re-
" flection in inebriating potions. The
" injuries and insults to which my o-
" dious profession exposed me eradi-
" cated from my heart every remain-
" ing human feeling. I became a mon-
" ster, cruel, relentless, ferocious; and
" contaminated alike, with a deadly poi-
" son, the health and the principles of
" those unfortunate victims whom, with
" practised allurements, I entangled in
" my snares. Man, however vicious,
" however cruel, reaches not the de-
" pravity of a shameless woman. *De-*
" *spair* shuts not against him every a-
" venue to repentance, *despair* drives him
" not from human sympathies; *despair*
' hurls him not from hope, from pity,
" from life's common charities, to plunge
" him into desperate, damned, guilt.
" ' Let

" ' Let the guileful feducer paufe here,
" and tremble! Let the fordid volup-
" tuary, the thoughtlefs libertine, ftop,
" amidft his felfifh gratifications, and
" reflect! Oh! let him balance this
" tremendous price, this deplorable ruin,
" againft the revel of an hour, the re-
" vel over which fatiety hovers, and to
" which difguft and laffitude quickly
" fucceed! Boaft not, vain man, of ci-
" vil refinements, while, in the bofom of
" thy moft polifhed and populous cities, an
" evil is foftered, poifoning virtue at its
" fource, diffufing through every rank its
" deadly venom, burfting the bonds of
" nature, blafting its endearments, deftroy-
" ing the promife of youth, the charm of
" domeftic affections, and hurling its hap
" lefs victims to irremediable perdition.
                              " ' The

" ' The evening, which completed
" my career of crime, roufed my flum-
" bering confcience. To *murder* I was
" yet unfamiliarized. In the inflant
" when remorfe, with its ferpent-fting,
" transfixed my heart, I beheld, with
" unfpeakable confufion and anguifh,
" the man who had, with honourable
" tendernefs, fought the chafle affec-
" tions of my youth. A thoufand poi-
" gnant emotions rufhed upon my foul:
" regret, fhame, terror, contrition, com-
" bined to convulfe my enfeebled frame.
" Through the dead filence of the night,
" amidft the prifon's gloom, contending
" paffions rent my tortured fpirit. in
" the bitternefs of defpair, I dafhed my
" wretched body againft the dungeon's
" floor; tore, with my nails, my hair, my
" flefh,

" flesh, my garments, groaned, howled,
" shrieked, in frantic agony. Towards
" morning, a stream of blood gushed
" from my nose and lips, and, mingling
" with a flood of tears, a kindly and
" copious shower, recalled me from the
" verge of insanity. The first collected
" thought which returning sense present-
" ed was, a determination to avoid the
" man whose value I had learned too
" late, and by whom I had been be-
" loved in my days of peace and in-
" nocence. I procured, as the day ad-
" vanced, the implements of writing,
" and traced the characters delivered to
" your hand, presaging, but too truly,
" your humane solicitude.

" ' At this period, I felt suddenly a-
" wakened, as it were, to a new ex-
　　　　　　　　　　　" istence.

" iftence. The profpect of death, by
" bounding the 'future, threw my ' re-
" flections upon the paft. I indulged
" in the mournful retrofpect; I com-
" mitted it to paper, while, as my
" thoughts were methodized, my fpirit
" became ferene.

" 'Lowly and tranquil, I await my
" deftiny, but feel, in the moment that
" life is cut fhort, difpofitions fpring-
" ing and powers expanding, that, per-
" mitted to unfold themfelves, might
" yet make reparation to the fociety I
" have injured, and on which I have
" but too well retaliated my wrongs.
" But it is too late! *Law* completes
" the triumph of injuftice. The def-
" potifm of man rendered me weak,
" his vices betrayed me into fhame, a
" barbarous

" barbarous policy ftifled returning dig-
" nity, prejudice robbed me of the means
" of independence, gratitude enfnared
" me in the devices of treachery, the
" contagion of example corrupted my
" heart, defpair hardened and brutality
" rendered it cruel. A fanguinary po-
" licy precludes reformation, defeating
" the dear-bought leffons of experience,
" and, by a legal procefs, affuming
" the aim of omnipotence, annihilates
" the being whom its negligence left
" deftitute, and its inftitutions compelled
" to offend.

" ' Thou, alfo, it may be, art in-
" capable of diftinction; thou, too, pro-
" bably, haft bartered the ingenuous
" virtues, the fenfibility of youth, for
" the defpotifm, the arrogance, the vo-
" luptuoufnefs,

" luptuoufnefs of man, and the un-
" fortunate daughter of an abandoned
" and wretched mother will fpread to
" thee her innocent arms in vain. If,
" amidft the corruption of vaunted ci-
" vilization, thy heart can yet throb
" refponfive to the voice of nature,
" and yield to the claims of huma-
" nity, fnatch from deftruction the child
" of an illicit commerce, fhelter her in-
" fant purity from contagion, guard her
" helplefs youth from a pitilefs world,
" cultivate her reafon, make her feel
" her nature's worth, ftrengthen her fa-
" culties, inure her to fuffer hardfhip,
" roufe her to independence, infpire
" her with fortitude, with energy, with
" felf-refpect, and teach her to contemn
" the tyranny that would impofe fetters
" of fex upon mind.   " ' MARY."

VOL. I.   I   Mr.

Mr. Raymond, in continuation: —

" The cover of thefe papers con-
" tained directions whereby I might
" trace the unhappy orphan thus fo-
" lemnly committed to my charge: it
" was thee, my beloved Mary! child
" of infamy and calamity! whom I ref-
" cued from the hovel of poverty and
" difgrace! I wept over thy infant
" beauties; I treafured up the dying
" precepts of thy ill-fated mother, I
" watched thy childhood with tender
" care, and nurtured thee with more
" than parental folicitude. It is now
" that I expect to reap the harveft of
" my cares, now is the critical period
" arrived on which hangs the future
" deftiny of my child. In the eye of
                              " the

" the world, the misfortunes of your
" birth stain your unsullied youth: it is
" in the dignity of your own mind that
" you must seek resource. The father
" of your lover has deeply imbibed these
" barbarous prejudices: the character of
" the son is yet wavering, his virtue un-
" tried, his principles unformed. Should
" he forfeit the privileges of his birth and
" rank, — should he contemn the daz-
" zling advantages which fortune pre-
" sents to him, — should he, impelled
" by the fervent passions of youth, im-
" pose upon himself fetters which, once
" rivetted, death only can dissolve, —
" will avarice, will ambition, never re-
" vive in his heart? will he live un-
" tainted in the midst of contagion? will
" established customs and sanctioned opi-
" nions, will the allurements of pleasure

" and

" and the deceptions of fashion, assail in
" vain his flexible youth? will he, a-
" midst the contempt of his equals, the
" scorn of his superiors, support a vir-
" tuous and rational singularity? will
" William Pelham, in the heart of a pro-
" fligate age, act the beardless philoso-
" pher? will he never become *a man of*
" *the world?* will he never curse the
" charms that blinded him to his inte-
" rest? and may not the sensible, the
" virtuous, the high-souled, Mary, per-
" ceive herself, when too late, the in-
" sulted wife of the man she loves?

" RAYMOND." —

CHAP.

C H A P. XIII.

I PERUSED this fatal narrative with mingled and indescribable emotion. I re-perused it: it was long ere I was capable of fully comprehending the consequences it involved: — by degrees they became unfolded to me in their extent; and this first lesson of injustice swelled my heart with indignant agony. It is thus that the principles of ingenuous youth, on his entrance into the world, become bewildered and shaken. Assailed by prejudice, betrayed by sophistry, distracted by contradiction, entangled in error, he exchanges the simple dictates of artless youth, the generous feelings of an uncorrupted heart,

I 3   the

the warm glow of natural affections, for the jargon of superstition, the frigid precautions of selfishness, the mask of hypocrisy, and the factitious distinctions of capricious folly: reason is perverted and fettered, and virtue polluted at its source.

I remained in my chamber for some hours, buried in thought, till I was roused from my reverie by some one softly opening the door. I started; the packet fell from my lap, and, on beholding William gazing earnestly in my face, (on which the recent traces of passion were legibly impressed,) with apparent surprise and concern, I burst into a convulsive flood of tears. Covering my face with my handkerchief, and pointing to the manuscript, which lay scattered teied on the floor, I rufhed by him, and fled precipitately from the apartment, while, having collected the papers, William ietiied with them to his chamber.

Feeling a fenfe of oppreffion, almoft to fuffocation, I quitted the houfe, and wandered, unconfcious of my path, into an adjoining copfe, till the night fhut in, dark and ftormy. The wind howled mournfully through the foliage, the leaves were fcattered at my feet, the rain fell in toiients, cold and chill; the underwood caught and rent my garments, which clung round me, heavy with the damps, and impeded my progrefs. I experienced, in encountering the conflicting elements, a gloomy fpecies of pleafure: they weie, methought, lefs

I 4 rude

rude and favage than barbarous man.
I recalled to my remembrance the i-
mage of my wretched mother: I beheld her, in idea, abandoned to infamy,
caft out of fociety, ftained with blood,
expiring on a fcaffold, unpitied and un-
wept.   I clafped my hands in agony,
terrors affailed me till then unknown,
the blood froze in my veins, a fhuddering horror crept through my heart,
when a low ruftling found, from an
adjoining thicket, fuddenly caught my
ftartled ear, while a pale light gleamed
at intervals through the trees. Liften-
ing, in fearful, undefinable, expectancy,
my breath grew fhort, my heart palpitated laborioufly, feeming to fwell to
my throat, as I effayed in vain to fhriek.
The founds at length became more diftinct; hafty footfteps approached, while,

fatigued

fatigued with unufual exertion, chilled by the hoftile elements, which every moment grew more tempeftuous, agitated by terrible and namelefs emotions, exhaufted by the ftruggle of warring paffions, my ftrength and my fpirits utterly failed, and I funk without motion on the turf.

Returning, in a few moments, to life and recollection, I found myfelf in the arms of my lover, accompanied by Mr. Neville, and a fervant carrying a light, to affift them in their fearch through the dark and pathlefs wildernefs, where, alarmed by my unufual abfence, and the inclemency of the weather, they had, for fome time, fought me in vain.

" For

" For God's fake! my dear Mifs
" Raymond!" exclaimed my hoft, in
a tone of mingled kindnefs and reproach, " what could induce you to pro-
" long your walk in a night like this?
" You know not the anxiety you have
" caufed us."

" I thank you," replied I, in a faint
voice, " for your friendly concern. I
" had, I believe, miffed my path."

William's eyes were fixed earneftly
upon mine. Withdrawing myfelf from
his arms, which ftill fupported me, and
accepting the aid of Mr. Neville, I returned with languid fteps towards the
houfe. Mrs. Neville, on our entrance,
haftened to meet us, full of folicitude

on my account. Obferving in my countenance the traces of unufual emotion,
fhe accofted me with tender fympathy,
preffing me to retire, and take that repofe which I fo evidently required. At-
tending me to my chamber, fhe affifted
in difengaging me from my wet garments. A torpid pain oppreffed my
head, laffitude and reftleffnefs feized my
limbs, cold fhiverings, fucceeded by a
feverifh diforder, confined me for fome
days to my apartment. During my in-
difpofition, I was attended by my hoftefs with maternal care. Affuring her
that my diforder would be but tranfient,
I fought to calm her inquietude, and
obtained from her a promife that my
guardian, without a material and threatening change, fhould not be alarmed by
the knowledge of my fituation.

My

My lover, abandoning himfelf for
fome days to the moft lively affliction,
would not be excluded from my chamber, fitting or kneeling whole hours in
filence near the feet of my bed, his
arms folded, and his features expreffive
of the moft poignant grief. My diforder at length abating, my fpirits grew
more tranquil. At my earneft requeft,
William was prevailed upon to quit my
apartment, and to content himfelf with
fhort occafional vifits and frequent inquiries. In my prefent feeble ftate, I convinced him, the difcompofure I fuffered
from his prefence was peculiarly injurious. I folicited and obtained from
him the return of the fatal packet,
which I had promifed to confide to
my kind hoftefs, and I engaged, on my
recovery,

recovery, to difcufs with him its contents.

During my ftate of convalefcence, I had time for reflection. The languor remaining from the effects of my illnefs abated the fervour of my feelings: the endearing tendernefs of my friend, who, with lively fympathy, interefted herfelf in my fituation, her judicious counfels, and animated approbation of my principles and conduct, aided, flattered, and foothed, me, while her experience enlightened me refpecting the nature of thofe cuftoms of which I had previoufly formed but a confufed apprehenfion. My refolutions every hour acquired ftrength, and my mind regained its vigour: I became infpired with an emulation to prove myfelf worthy the confidence of my patron,

tron, who, fatisfied with having communicated to me the circumftances which rendered my deftiny peculiar, trufted for my conduct to the principles he had impreffed upon my mind, principles, of which he had a right to expect the fruits.

CHAP.

CHAP. XIV.

MY lover grew impatient for the promifed conference; a conference, how
dreaded foever, which, my health being
now nearly re-eftablifhed, I had no longer any pretence to avoid.

"Why," faid he, in a tone of reproach, as he entered the parlour, where
I waited in agitation his approach, "why
"am I excluded from your prefence?
"Why, when we meet, thofe averted
"eyes, that cold and diftant air? Can
"it be that the tender, the fenfible,
"Mary hefitates whether to facrifice
"the man who adores her, the man
"whom fhe has a thoufand times pro-
"feffed

" feffed to love, to a fenfelefs chimera,
" an odious tyranny, againft which rea-
" fon indignantly revolts, or does fhe
" delight to torture the heart, over which
" fhe is but too well affured of her
" power?"

" Alas, my friend!" replied I, regarding him with melancholy earneftnefs,
and gently placing my hand on his,
which he vehemently fnatched to his
lips, " wound not my heart by thefe
" injurious reproaches. It is true that
" *I love you*, tenderly love you: God
" knows how dear you are to me,
" and the anguifh it cofts me to be
" compelled to renounce you! God
" knows that, in rending fiom my heart
" the fentiment fo cherifhed, the fenti-
" ment that has fo long conftituted its
" happinefs,

" happinefs, I part with all that endears
" life !"

" Why, then, do violence to that in-
" valuable heart? Why not liften to
" its juft and gentle dictates?"

" Need I recall to your mind" (covering my face with my handkerchief)
" the tale which has harrowed up my
" own? Ah, William! can I, ought
" I, to bring difhonour as my only
" dowry to the arms of the man I
" love?"

" You deceive yourfelf, Mary, when
" you would adopt the language which
" truth and nature alike abhor. Beau-
" ty, virtue, talents, derive honour from
" no flation, and confer it upon all.
" Can

" Can a mind enlightened, a spirit dig-
" nified, as your's, submit to a tyranny
" thus fantaftic?"

" I do not deny that I am fenfible
" of its injuftice, an injuftice that my
" reafon and my affections equally con-
" temn ; yet who am I, that I fhould
" refift the united voice of mankind,
" that I fhould oppofe a judgement im-
" mature and inexperienced againft the
" cuftoms which ufe has fanctioned, and
" expedience, it may be, confirmed ?"

" Are thefe the magnanimous prin-
" ciples, is this the fortitude, that blend-
" ed refpect with tendernefs, that left my
" heart in doubt whether the paffion you
" infpired ———— "

" Ah!

" Ah! I know too well all you would
" urge : I dare not trust your pleadings ;
" I dread left I should mistake the te-
" merity of passion for the dictates of
" principle, left I should purchafe pre-
" fent gratification at the expenfe of fu-
" ture remorfe."

" And what is the dreaded, the chi-
" merical, evil, to avert which demands
" this expenfive facrifice ; to which you
" thus lavifhly offer up our deareft
" hopes ? — Duty, virtue, happinefs,
" form an indiffoluble bond. Can it be
" you, rafh, but charming, maid! who
" feek, by factitious diftinctions, to dif-
" folve the facred union ?"

" Our

" Our fituations, our claims, our prof-
" pects, thus widely differing, dare I en-
" tail upon you evils to which your firm-
" nefs and your recompenfe might, alas!
" be unequal?"

" You love me not:" (his cheeks
glowing and his eyes flashing fire:) " did
" you love me, thefe fufpicions, fo un-
" worthy of yourfelf and your lover,
" would have no place in your heart.   I
" perceive but too plainly that you dif-
" truft and defpife me!"

" My friend! my beloved friend!
" your emotion afflicts, but does not
" offend me.   Have pity on my weak-
" nefs, on my youth, my fex.   My
" heart finks under the tafk impofed
                                " upon

" upon it: in afflicting you, heaven
" knows the anguish it endures. Dif-
" tinguish, I entreat you, distinguish
" between our various duties. In me,
" it is virtue to submit to a destiny,
" however painful, not wilfully incur-
" red, and, in all that affects myself
" merely, to rise magnanimously above
" it: but why should *you* expose your-
" self to a doubtful conflict and a cer-
" tain penalty?—The confidence which
" in you is generous, in me would change
" its nature, and, in its failure, entail
" upon me a double portion of remorse
" and shame.—William, dear William,
" turn not thus from me! Your dif-
" pleasure pierces my soul."

" My dearest girl! distract me not
" thus with contradictions and refine-
" ments;

" ments, suffer not the simplicity of
" your mind to be perverted and de-
" bauched by factitious sophisms, do
" not yield our mutual happiness to the
" subtleties of a fantastic theory."

" Answer me, my friend, and answer
" me truly, dare you believe that your
" father, tenacious of the honour of an
" unsullied name, would consent to our
" union, would consent to enrol a daugh-
" ter of infamy in a family vain of il-
" lustrious descent? Have the habits
" of your youth inured you to labour?
" have they prepared you for indepen-
" dence? Have reprobation, poverty,
" disgrace, the contumely of the world,
" however unmerited, no terrors for
" William Pelham? Will he forfeit
" the privileges of his rank and birth?
　　　　　　　　　　" Will

" Will he, for the fmiles of love, brave
" the frowns of foitune, and, in the
" decay of thofe charms, which owe to
" youth and novelty their glofs, will he
" never repent, will he never curfe, the
" fafcination which mifled him to his
" ruin?"

" Why thus conjure up phantoms for
" our mutual toiture? Where is the
" neceffity for combating evils thus for-
" midably and fancifully arrayed? The
" cruel narrative, that has wounded your
" gentle nature, is probably known but
" to ourfelves: the village believes you
" the relation of your pation, my fa-
" ther knows you foi no other. by a
" prudent filence, the confequences of
" its difclofuie might yet be aveit-
" ed. My father loves me: he is
                                        " not

" not fordid : why fhould we roufe in
" his heart this idol, honour? Is it
" virtue to facrifice to the fhrine of
" prejudice, however venerable or im-
" pofing its claims ?"

" Dare you then believe that my
" guardian, whofe ftern integrity bends
" to no expedients, could be prevailed
" upon to fofter the deceit? On a fub-
" ject thus interefting, would Mr Pel-
" ham make no inquiries, fhould we
" confent to unite in a wilful prevari-
" cation? Is there no caufe to fear left
" the voice of rumour, that blazons
" the tale of fhame, fhould bear the
" cruel tidings to his ear ?"

" What is the value of *truth*, ab-
" ftracted from its expedience ? — Vir-

" tue

" tue itfelf is worthlefs but as a mean to
" *happinefs.*"

" Ah! beware of fophiftry and con-
" fcious perverfion! A prefent gratifi-
" cation in view, is there no danger of
" felfifh delufion? Is paffion an impar-
" tial judge of the propriety of violating
" moral fanctions? If, where intereft af-
" fails us, we fuffer our principles to
" yield, who can tell to what fearful
" lengths, on leffer occafions, a prece-
" dent thus pernicious may lead us! —
" Is a habit of rectitude broken with im-
" punity?"

" Good God!" exclaimed my lover,
with vehemence, " does *love* argue thus
" coolly when its deareft interefts are
" at ftake? You love me not! you ne-

VOL. I.   K   " ver

" ver loved me! Pride and fickleness
" have fortified your heart! It is vain
" to expect from woman a stability for
" which sex and nature have incapaci-
" tated her!"

" Unjust William! cruel as unjust!
" what but *love*, tender, powerful, felf-
" annihilating love,—that, where the wel-
" fare of the beloved object is at stake,
" triumphing in its sufferings, is content
" to be the victim,— could enable me to
" stifle the importunate yearnings of a
" fond and breaking heart? I perceive
" on every side, while I would ward
" them from *you*, the miseries which
" menace our ill-fated attachment. A
" dark cloud, surcharged with storms,
" hangs over my fate. Let it waste on
" me its fury. I dare to give you up,

" to

" to lofe, to renounce you. I can weep,
" and my forrow fhall be luxury; but
" I dare not, will not, confent to involve
" in my deftiny the man I love, — to
" become at once his misfortune and his
" curfe."

My exhaufted fpirits would no longer
fuftain me: my head funk on my bofom, my tears flowed without control.
My lover knelt at my feet, folded me to
his bofom, tenderly embraced me, mingling his tears with mine, and at length
wrung from me a promife that I would
confent to be his, if, after difclofing to
his father, without referve, the particulars of my birth, he could, by expof-
tulation or entreaties, extort from him
even a reluctant confent. He affured
himfelf, with the fanguine ardour of

youth

youth and inexperience, that every scruple muſt be vanquiſhed by the powerful and united eloquence of nature, love, and truth.

I liſtened to his rapturous exultations in mournful ſilence. I returned to him the papers of Mr. Raymond. Separating myſelf from him with difficulty, I retired to my chamber, whither I was followed by my kind hoſteſs. Repeating to her the particulars of the paſt conflict, I ſought relief in her tender ſympathy.

Early in the enſuing morning, William departed for the metropolis. I preſaged but too well the iſſue of his romantic project, and a fearful deſpondency gradually pervaded my mind.

CHAP.

CHAP. XV.

ON the following day, as my thoughts became more collected, I took up my pen, and, addreffing myfelf to Mr. Raymond, made him a faithful recital of the circumftances which had fucceeded the receipt of his affecting narrative. I poured out my heart to this invaluable friend without referve, and befought his future counfel.

" You have fulfilled, my deareft
" child," faid he, in his reply to my
appeal, " my moft fanguine expecta-
" tion. Continue to act up to the dic-
" tates of your own admirable judge-
" ment: if I had not affifted you in

K 3   " forming

" forming principles of rectitude, and
" in acquiring courage to put them in
" practice, I should not now dare to
" add, to the crime of negligence, the
" tyranny of control. It is *you* who
" are to decide on the materials laid
" before you; but do not misconstrue
" the ground of my solicitude, there
" is no contradiction in the principles
" I would inculcate. Your affection
" for William Pelham, not more na-
" tural than laudable, has hitherto pro-
" duced upon your character the hap-
" piest effects: virtuous tenderness pu-
" rifies the heart, carries forward the
" understanding, refines the passions,
" dignifies the feelings, and raises hu-
" man nature to its sublimest standard
" of excellence. I rejoice in your ca-
" pacity for these admirable sensibili-
" ties,

" ties; but, when I perceive you ex-
" alted, but not enflaved by them, I
" exult and glory in my child! Wil-
" liam's youth, inexperience, inftabi-
" lity, and habits of dependence, are
" the only reafonable obftacles which
" oppofe your mutual wifhes: fhould
" his attachment prove worthy its ob-
" ject, thefe obftacles, though threat-
" ening, are far from infuperable. His
" deftiny will not permit us to con-
" fine him in rural fhades: let him try
" the world, and prove his boafted
" ftrength: if, in the arduous warfare,
" victory crown his efforts, let him
" return, and claim the recompenfe of
" his toils: the invaluable heart of my
" child will be a victor's rich re-
" ward.

" I

" I yearn to clafp my beloved Mary,
" the pride and comfort of my declining
" years, to my paternal bofom.   In her
" happinefs and improvement, my hopes
" and affections fondly centre.

" RAYMOND."

The concluding paragraph of this letter determined me on an immediate return to the beloved afylum of my childhood.   The neceffity for my abfence no
longer exifted : I longed to embrace my
father and my friend, to bafk in the fun-
fhine of his approving fmiles.   After acquainting my friends with my intention,
I began with alacrity to prepare for my
departure.

The

The evening previous to the day appointed for my journey, a letter was brought by a horseman to the parsonage, superscribed to Miss Raymond. I had strayed into the meadows adjoining the orchard, and met, on my return, my hostess, who had been seeking me, and who put into my hand the paper left by the messenger. I trembled and changed colour on recognizing the well-known writing of my lover. Hastily breaking the seal, I read the following lines: —

" *To* Miss Raymond.

" Your mistaken heroism has ruined
" us! My father is inexorable! He
" is preparing to send me to the con-
" tinent, whither Edmund is, for the
" benefit of his health, advised to re-

K 5   " pair.

" pair. Two years is the period al-
" lotted for our abfence. I am deter-
" mined to refift this tyranny, and brave
" every confequence. I fhall follow my
" letter immediately, and once more
" tender to you my heart and hand :
" if you are then refolved rather to o-
" bey the dictates of a frigid prudence
" than yield to the united claims of
" virtue, love, and reafon, you will pro-
" bably regret in future the effects of
" a defpair for which *you* only will be re-
" fponfible.   " W. P."

The fortitude I had been ftruggling
to attain forfook me on the perufal of
this epiftle. I gave it, without fpeaking,
to my friend, and, clafping my arms
round her neck, funk, half-fainting, on
her maternal bofom. She fupported me

                                        to

to my chamber, and, remaining with me
till the night was far fpent, fought by
every endearment to calm the perturbation of my fpirits. Quitting me towards
morning, fhe entreated me to endeavour
to take fome repofe. In compliance
with her folicitude, I threw myfelf, in
my clothes, on the bed, but reft fled
from me. As the day dawned, abandoning my pillow, and foftly ftealing
from my chamber, I panted to relieve
my overcharged heart by breathing a
freer air. Opening the door which led
into the garden, I wandered through the
enclofures, and, at length, wearied and
exhaufted, feated myfelf on a ruftic bench,
at the foot of an aged oak, where I
watched the crimfon clouds, the harbin-
gers of day. Abforbed in reflection, the
hours paffed unheeded, and the fun rofe

high

high above the horizon ere I quitted my
retreat.

I returned flowly towards the houfe,
and, on entering the parlour, beheld,
with furprife and emotion, my lover in
earneft converfation with Mrs. Neville,
his drefs negligent and his air wild and
perturbed. He turned fuddenly, on my
entrance, and, obferving my pallid countenance, tottering fteps, and features on
which the ravages of paffion were impreffed, folded me to his bofom, and,
by the mute eloquence of affectionate
endearment, expreffed his tender fympathy. The entrance of Mr. Neville
prevented for the prefent any explana-
tion of our fentiments. During the re-
paft, I tried to rally my fainting fpirits, and to prepare myfelf for the approaching

proaching trial. I recalled to my remembrance every confideration which
might tend to fortify my conduct and
control my feelings, while I fought in
vain to roufe my languid powers. Our
humane hoft but too well comprehending our fituation, on fome pretence,
breakfaft being ended, quitted the room.
Mrs. Neville was about to follow her
hufband, but, preventing her defign,
I entreated the fupport of her prefence.

In vain fhould I attempt to do juftice to the conflict which enfued: my
lover omitted no means to effect his
purpofe and affail my faultering refolution: he knelt, implored, argued, wept,
threatened, reproached, curfed himfelf,
his father, my patron, the whole world,

with

with terrible imprecations; gave a loose to all the impetuofity of his paffions; and abandoned himfelf to the moft frantic exceffes. Stunned, confounded, fhocked, overborne, my fenfes grew bewildered: I funk into a kind of ftupor, and became unconfcious to what was paffing. I neither fpoke nor wept; but, with a wild air, continued to gaze vacantly.

Mrs. Neville perceived my fituation; and, taking my cold and lifelefs hand, attempted to withdraw me from a fcene to which my faculties were no longer equal. She uttered, as fhe tried to roufe my attention, a fevere reprimand to my lover. He caught the alarm, checked himfelf, and, at her repeated folicitation, confented to withdraw, and

to

to postpone for the present what he had farther to urge.

It was not till after many hours, and a short but profound slumber, that I was capable of resuming the affecting subject. William, apprehensive for my health and intellects, had now become more moderate: he at length suffered himself to yield to our united reasonings, respecting the danger and impropriety of a precipitate conduct, in defiance of his father's injunctions, in a case thus important. I communicated to him the letter I had received from Mr. Raymond, wherein he generously confides in my judgement and prudence, and hints, that the barriers, which, at present, opposed themselves to our happiness, may yield to time and perseverance.

rance. I aſſured my lover, repeatedly and tenderly aſſured him, if, on his return from the continent, a commerce with the world had wrought no change in his affections; if, in the interval, he had determined on ſome plan of independence; if, when not wholly unacquainted with them, he perſiſted in deſpiſing the allurements of intereſt and ambition; if his preſent views and ſentiments were confirmed and ſanctioned by time and experience; he might then challenge my faith and affection, and I ſhould glory in aiding him to give an example to the world of the triumph of virtuous and unſophiſticated feelings.

Appeaſed, in ſome meaſure, by theſe repreſentations, he engaged in all things

to refign himfelf to my will, on condition that I would previoufly, as a
pledge of my fincerity, and to obviate
future hazards or plans for our feparation, fuffer the nuptial-ceremony to be
performed by Mr. Neville : in that cafe,
whatever it might coft him, he would
quit me immediately after the fervice,
would go abroad, remain there the al-
lotted period, and endeavour to wait
patiently a prudent feafon for the difclo-
fure of our marriage.

"Do you not perceive, my friend,"
replied I, "the inconfiftency, the ab-
"furdity, of this plan? —— What!
"fhall I firft bind my fate to your's,
"and then fuffer you, far from the in-
"fluence of my tender, watchful, af-
"fection, to expofe your yet-uncer-
"tain

" tain virtue to the contagion of the
" world?"

" Promife me, then," interrupted he,
with vehemence, " promife that, in my
" abfence, you will liften to no other
" propofals: I forefee the trials to which
" your conftancy will be expofed; every
" man who beholds will love you, will
" be my rival."

" If your knowledge of my heart af-
" ford you not a fecurity for my faith,
" weak indeed were the fanction of
" oaths, and unworthy the facred flame
" that animates us: were not your fears
" as injurious as chimerical, would you
" accept the cold reluctant hand, the
" victim of fuperftition, when the alien-
" ated mind deplored the facrifice? No,
                              " William:

" William! I will neither give nor re-
" ceive vows: let us both be free, and
" let our re-union be the cheerful, vo-
" luntary, dignified, confummation of
" love and virtue."

The day wore away before the fcruples
of my lover were vanquifhed: the con-
tention was long and arduous: I fuffered
not my friend to quit me for a moment,
diftrufting the fpirit for which I had fo
painfully ftruggled. Our parting was
tender and mournful: my lover quitting
me, and returning again and again to take
a laft embrace, protracted the agony of
feparation. The next day and the day
following, wholly abforbed in grief, I
was unable to quit my chamber: my
benefactor, my home, every idea but
one

one feemed entirely effaced from my remembrance.

END OF THE FIRST VOLUME.

CPSIA information can be obtained at www.ICGtesting.com
Printed in the USA
LVOW02s2324291113

363233LV00024B/1613/P